Instructor's Manual
for

Ramage • Bean

WRITING ARGUMENTS
FOURTH EDITION

Kathy Overhulse Smith
Indiana University

Allyn and Bacon
Boston · London · Toronto · Sydney · Tokyo · Singapore

Copyright © 1998 by Allyn & Bacon
A Viacom Company
Needham Heights, Massachusetts 02194

Internet: www.abacon.com
America Online: keyword: College Online

All rights reserved. The contents, or parts thereof, may be reproduced for use with *Writing Arguments,* Fourth Edition, by John D. Ramage and John C. Bean, provided such reproductions bear copyright notice, but may not be reproduced in any form for any other purpose without written permission from the copyright owner.

ISBN 0-205-27246-0

Printed in the United States of America

10 9 8 7 6 5 4 3 2 1   01 00 99 98 97

TABLE OF CONTENTS

I. GENERAL ISSUES IN USING THIS TEXT   1

THE "PROCESS" APPROACH TO TEACHING ARGUMENT: INTEGRATING THE "PROCESS OF ARGUING" WITH THE "PROCESS OF WRITING"   1

A RATIONALE FOR THE GENERAL STRUCTURE   1

DESCRIPTION OF WRITING ASSIGNMENTS   5

CREATING A SYLLABUS FOR THE COURSE   9
- Deciding on Writing Assignments for the Course   9
- Deciding on Your Use of Class Time   12
- Deciding on Textbook Materials to be Covered   12

A SAMPLE SYLLABUS FOR A FRESHMAN COURSE USING THE ALTERNATIVE ASSIGNMENT SEQUENCE THAT INCLUDES THE <u>STASES</u> CHAPTERS (PART THREE)   13

HOW THIS TEXT TREATS "INVENTION"   15

USING <u>FOR CLASS DISCUSSION</u> EXERCISES AS COLLABORATIVE LEARNING TASKS   15
- Design of Collaborative Tasks   16
- Dividing the Class into Collaborative Groups   16
- Instructor's Role During the Collaborative Task   18
- Instructor's Role During the Plenary Session   18

USING COLLABORATIVE GROUPS FOR WRITING PROCESS WORKSHOPS   19
- Using Collaborative Groups for Invention, and Exploration   19
- Using Collaborative Groups for Revision   19

Using Collaborative Groups for Editing 21

SUGGESTIONS FOR TEACHING THE TOULMIN SYSTEM 21

How and Why We Have Added Enthymemic Language to Toulmin's System 22

Why We Use Toulmin: The Evolution of Our Approach to Argument 26

A Classroom Strategy for Teaching Toulmin 28

What About Messy Student Examples of Enthymemes that Don't "Fit" Toulmin's Schema? 32

II. SUGGESTED ANSWERS TO FOR CLASS DISCUSSION EXERCISES 35

CHAPTER 1	35
CHAPTER 2	37
CHAPTER 3	39
CHAPTER 4	45
CHAPTER 5	47
CHAPTER 6	51
CHAPTER 7	52
CHAPTER 8	55
CHAPTER 9	57
CHAPTER 10	59
CHAPTER 11	62
CHAPTER 12	65
CHAPTERS 13-17	68
APPENDIX ONE	71
APPENDIX TWO	73

III. CRITERIA CHECKLISTS FOR PEER REVIEW OF DRAFTS 78

GENERAL CHECKLIST FOR EVALUATING DRAFTS 78

CHECKLISTS FOR THE FIVE STASES OF ARGUMENTS 80

  Definition Arguments (Chapter 10) 80

  Cause/Consequence Arguments (Chapter 11) 81

  Resemblance Arguments (Chapter 12) 82

  Evaluation Arguments (Chapter 13) 83

  Proposal Arguments (Chapter 14) 84

  Ethical Arguments (Chapter 15) 85

IV. ANALYSIS OF THE READINGS 86

ESSAYS FROM CHAPTER 10 (DEFINITION) 86

  Kathy Sullivan, "Oncore, Obscenity, and the Liquor Control Board" (pp. 220-221) 86

  Charles Krauthammer, "How to Save the Homeless Mentally Ill" (pp. 221-227) 88

ESSAYS FROM CHAPTER 11 (CAUSE/CONSEQUENCE) 89

  Carl Sagan, "Warming of the World" (pp. 253-257) 89

  Victor Fuchs, "Why Married Women Work" (pp. 259-262) 90

  Mary Lou Torpey, "What Drugs I Take Is None of Your Business" (pp. 257-258) 92

  Walter Minot, "Students Who Push Burgers" (pp. 262-263) 92

ESSAY FROM CHAPTER 12 (RESEMBLANCE)   93

   Susan Brownmiller, "Against Our Will: Men, Women and Rape" (pp. 278-280)   93

ESSAYS FROM CHAPTER 13 (EVALUATION)   94

   Murray Weidenbaum, "How to Reform the Federal Tax System: Just the Basics, Please" (pp. 297-298)   94

   Terry Tang, "Clinton Can Show Courage by Vetoing Bad Welfare Bill" (pp. 298-299)   95

   Sam Isaacson, "Would Legalization of Gay Marriage Be Good for the Gay Community?" (pp. 300-302)   96

   Debra Goodwin, "Beauty Pageant Fallacies" (pp. 302-303)   98

ESSAYS FROM CHAPTER 14 (PROPOSAL)   99

   Jeffrey Cain, "A Proposal to Save Bernie's Blintzes Restaurant" (pp. 323-329)   99

   Stephen Bean, "What Should Be Done About the Mentally Ill Homeless?" (pp. 330-338)   101

ESSAY FROM CHAPTER 15 (ETHICAL ARGUMENTS)   103

   Ursula Le Guin, "The Ones Who Walk Away from Omelas" (pp. 349-353)   103

ESSAY FROM CHAPTER 17 (USING AND DOCUMENTING SOURCES)   104

   Michael Levin, "The Case for Torture" (pp. 387-389)   104

V. ANALYSIS OF ESSAYS FROM PART FIVE: AN ANTHOLOGY OF ARGUMENTS   105

IMMIGRATION POLICY   106
Julian Simon, "The Case for Greatly Increased Immigration"

Michael Lind, "Huddled Excesses"

Dan Stein, "Timeout: The United States Needs a Moratorium on Immigration"

MERCY KILLING AND THE RIGHT TO DIE   111
James Rachels, "Active and Passive Euthanasia"

David B. McCurdy, "Saying What We Mean"

William May, "Rising to the Occasion of Our Death"

THE RESPONSIBILITY OF THE RICH FOR THE POOR   116
Garret Hardin, "Lifeboat Ethics: The Case Against Helping the Poor"

Peter Singer, "Rich and Poor"

CIVIL DISOBEDIENCE   121
Martin Luther King, Jr. "Letter from Birmingham Jail"

Lewis Van Dusen, "Civil Disobedience: Destroyer of Democracy"

Plato, from <u>The Crito</u>

CENSORSHIP ON THE INTERNET   125
Mike Romano, "In Defense of Decency"

Kathleen Durkan, "Net Benefit"

Marc Rothenberg, "The Net Doesn't Need Thought Police"

Senator James Exon, "Only the Force of Law Can Deter Pornographers"

James Gleick, "This is Safe Sex?"

LEGALIZATION OF DRUGS 130

Michael Gazzaniga (Interview), "The Federal Drug Store"

Walter Wink, "Biting the Bullet: The Case for Legalizing Drugs"

Richard J. Dennis, "The Economics of Legalizing Drugs"

James Q. Wilson, "Against the Legalization of Drugs"

Lee N. Robins, Darlene H. Davis, and Donald W. Goodwin, "Drug Use by U.S. Army Enlisted Men in Vietnam: A Follow-Up on Their Return Home"

SEXUAL HARASSMENT 138

Stephanie Riger, "Gender Dilemmas in Sexual Harassment Policies and Procedures"

Naomi Munson, "Harassment Blues"

Erica Jong, "Fear of Flirting"

Gretchen Morgenson, "Watch the Leer, Stifle That Joke"

Susan Crawford, "A Wink Here, a Leer There: It's Costly"

Martha Chamallas, "Universal Truth and Multiple Perspectives: Controversies on Sexual Harassment"

RECYCLING AND GARBAGE 143

Patricia Poore, "America's 'Garbage Crisis': A Toxic Myth"

Chris Hendrickson, Lester Lavbe, Francis McMichael, "Time to Dump Recycling"

Robert Steuteville, "Don't Dump Recycling"

Reid Lifset and John Schall, "Response to Hendrickson et al."

Brenda Platt and Neil Seldman, "Response to Hendrickson et al."

Lynn Scarlett, "Recycling: Asking the Right Questions"

Nancy Glaser, "Recycling: The Other Coast, the Other Story"

SOCIAL POLICY TOWARD THE HOMELESS
MENTALLY ILL 149
Paul S. Appelbaum, "Crazy in the Streets"

Jonathan Kozol, "Are the Homeless Crazy?"

Steven Vanderstaay, "The Homeless Mentally Ill"

E. Torrey Fuller, "Who Goes Homeless?"

SAME-SEX MARRIAGE 154
Andrew Sullivan, "Here Comes the Groom: A (Conservative) Case for Gay Marriage"

Dennis O'Brien, "Against Gay Marriage--I: What Heterosexuality Means"

John Leo, "Gay Rights, Gay Marriage"

Jonathan Rauch, "For Better or Worse? The Case for Gay (and Straight) Marriage"

FAMILY VALUES, SINGLE PARENTHOOD, AND
WELFARE REFORM 160
Katha Pollit, "Why I Hate 'Family Values' (Let Me Count the Ways)"

Elijah Anderson, "Abolishing Welfare Won't Stop Poverty"

Barbara Defoe Whitehead, "Dan Quayle Was Right"

VI. SELECTED BIBLIOGRAPHY OF WORKS ON ARGUMENT 165

I. GENERAL ISSUES IN USING THIS TEXT

THE "PROCESS" APPROACH TO TEACHING ARGUMENT: INTEGRATING THE "PROCESS OF ARGUING" WITH THE "PROCESS OF WRITING"

The basic premise of this textbook is that writing and arguing are closely related processes. In this regard, we share composition theorist Ann Berthoff's view that the act of composing is a dialogic process in which writers learn to role-play opposing voices, to carry on a dialogue with themselves as they shuttle back and forth between the generation of ideas and the critical assessment of those ideas. We see both the act of writing and the act of arguing as a journey toward conclusions that often can't be foreseen.

Argument, to us, is not a way of rationalizing claims to which we are committed before the act of arguing occurs. Rather, argument is a process of exploring various points of view in order to arrive gradually at the best conclusions. Hence our emphasis on <u>clarification</u> as an important goal of argument. When argument is treated as product in this text, it is seen as a final persuasive presentation of a position arrived at through argument as process. In Chapter 1, therefore, we envision a well-functioning committee as a model for the arguing process. The classroom equivalent of the well-functioning committee is the collaborative group. Throughout the text, the numerous <u>For Class Discussion</u> exercises provide opportunities for collaborative group work. (Teachers who wish to use collaborative learning in the classroom may wish to assign Appendix Two early in the course.)

A RATIONALE FOR THE STRUCTURE OF THIS TEXT
<u>Writing Arguments</u>, 4th edition, is divided into five main parts and two appendices as follows:

Part One: "Overview of Argument"
Part One, combined with Part Two, forms a self-contained mini-text suitable for a freshman course in argument. Indeed some teachers will choose to emphasize just these two parts for a freshman course, especially if the course is offered on the quarter system.

Part One (Chapters 1-3) is introductory. These chapters present our notion of argument as a process of clarification and, in Chapters 2 and 3, link the process of arguing to the process of reading and writing. Chapter 2 treats reading as an active meaning-making activity drawing on students' capacity, which needs to be nurtured, of believing and doubting. Particularly, the chapter teaches students how to write summaries as a means of "listening" to arguments and how to raise questions about facts, definitions, values, and analogies as a means of maintaining critical distance. Chapter 3 presents useful heuristics for argument and concludes with two exploratory sequences for helping students generate ideas for future papers.

Part Two: "Principles of Argument"
Part Two examines the principles of argument. Chapters 4-6 show that the core of an argument is a claim with reasons. These reasons are often stated as enthymemes, the unstated premise of which must sometimes be brought to the surface and supported. Discussion of Toulmin logic shows students how to discover both the stated and unstated premises of their arguments and to provide structures of reasons and evidence to support them. Chapters 7 and 8 focus on the rhetorical context of arguments. These chapters discuss the writer's relationship with an audience, particularly with finding audience-based reasons, with using <u>pathos</u> and <u>ethos</u> effectively and responsibly, and with accommodating or refuting opposing views.
The writing assignments following Parts One and Two provide a coherent sequence of tasks that build argumentative skills sequentially. A freshman course could be built entirely on these tasks.

Part Three: "Arguments in Depth: Five Categories of Claims"
Part Three treats five modes or <u>stases</u> of argument: definition, cause/consequence, resemblance, evaluation, and proposal, with a concluding chapter on special problems of moral arguments. We intend Part Three to be the heart of an advanced course in argument, although the material is certainly accessible to freshmen also and many teachers have used these chapters successfully in freshmen courses.
The stasis or modal approach employed in Part Three introduces students to three different kinds of argumentative

"moves" or thinking strategies that recur in various combinations in almost all arguments: (1) a criteria-match strategy in which one establishes criteria for defining or evaluating a given class Y and then argues that a specific X meets or does not meet the criteria; (2) a causal strategy in which one argues that X leads to Y; (3) and a resemblance strategy in which one argues through analogy or precedent that X is like Y. (For a more developed justification of the stasis or modal approach, see Fahnestock, Jeanne and Marie Secor, "Teaching Argument: A Theory of Types," CCC, 34 [February 1983], 20-30.)

These three argumentative "moves" are presented as a general heuristic for argument in Chapter 9 (arguments from principle, from cause/consequence, and from resemblance). Students then look at each mode of argument in more depth throughout Part Three.

The chief strength of a modal approach is its heuristic power and its systematic development of thinking and arguing skills. Its chief potential weakness is that students might come to expect all arguments to fit neatly into one of the modes. To obviate this problem, we treat the modes throughout as means of invention and exploration rather than as means of classification (see Frank D'Angelo's discussion of the connection between rhetorical forms and conceptual structures of cognition in A Conceptual Theory of Rhetoric, Cambridge, Mass.: Winthrop, 1975) and stress that most arguments involve shuttling back and forth among the modes.

We have integrated writing assignments into each of the five modal chapters in Part Three (Chapters 10-14). Each assignment offers students a variety of options by encouraging students to choose an issue-question that can be developed through the mode under discussion.

Part Four: "Writing from Sources: The Argument as a Formal Research Paper"

Part Four examines the research paper. Chapter 16 teaches students how to use a library and the Internet, particularly how to unlock the vast wealth of information that these resources contain and that writers of argument often need. Chapter 17 focuses on using and documenting sources. It covers all the conventional material about citations, documentation, plagiarism, and so forth, but it also focuses on how to use sources. It shows, for example, how two writers might summarize the same article in different ways to meet the rhetorical demands of different issue-questions or different claims.

For courses that end with a major research argument, we recommend a term project that grows out of Option 5 in "Writing Assignments for Chapters 1-3" (p. 77), which in turn is based on Task 3 in the "Starting Points" exploration sequence (p. 72)--"I am not sure where I stand on the issue of . . . " This option asks students to identify an issue of interest to them on which they are currently puzzled and undecided. The research project requires them to research the issue, weigh all sides, take a stand, and write a major argument supporting their position.

Appendices

The text has two appendices. The first treats informal logical fallacies and can be introduced at any stage in the course. The second discusses collaborative learning, including various strategies for working effectively in groups. It concludes with several group tasks: how to conduct a class "norming session" on arguments and how to conduct a classroom debate. This appendix could be introduced in conjunction with Chapter 3 at the point where we encourage students to talk about their ideas in small groups as one strategy for improving their writing processes.

Part Five: "An Anthology of Arguments"

Part Five provides a selection of professional arguments covering eleven topic areas. We have selected the essays in each of these topic areas with an eye toward representing a wide spectrum of views, suggesting the subtlety and complexity of arguments in the real world and consistent with our treatment of argument in the text as a multi-sided conversation rather than a pro-con debate. Additionally, throughout the rhetoric section of the text we have included several dozen additional arguments--both student and professional--that illustrate the strategies under discussion. Two of the topics raised in the rhetoric section (illegitimacy and single-parenthood from Chapter 2 and the mentally ill homeless in Chapters 10 and 14 are treated more fully in the anthology.)

Teachers will make different uses of these readings. Those who devote the majority of class time to student writing and the sharing of drafts might have only limited space for discussing readings. Such teachers might choose to use Part Five sparingly basing the course primarily on student writing rather than on reading and analysis of arguments.

Other teachers might use the anthology extensively. There are several ways to do so. The essays can be used to teach the process of reading arguments as discussed in Chapter 2. Analyzing why arguers disagree with each other--through disagreement about facts, definitions, analogies, or beliefs and values--is wonderful training in critical thinking and sophisticated reading.

Additionally, the essays can be used as sample arguments for close analysis. Following the strategies discussed throughout the text, students can examine the organization of the essays, the rhetorical strategies employed, the effectiveness of the argument's logos, the author's creation of ethos and pathos, and so forth. To aid the teacher using this approach, this Instructor's Manual includes our analyses of all the readings.

But probably the richest way to use the readings is as a stimulus for classroom discussion and debate. Task 5 in the "Starting Points" exploration assignments (p. 72) asks students to respond to one of the sets of essays by entering into an imagined conversation with the authors. This same strategy can be used for any of the argument groupings, thus involving students in sustained inquiry into the complexity of an issue. Optional writing assignments, usually set as "cases," follow each of the argument groupings. Teachers may choose to use these for some of the formal assignments in the course.

DESCRIPTION OF WRITING ASSIGNMENTS IN THE TEXT

The text provides many options for writing assignments, enabling instructors to create assignment sequences suitable to their needs and purposes. A summary of these assignments will help instructors get a quick overview of the available options.

<u>Exploration Tasks--Set 1: Starting Points</u> (pp. 71-73)

This set of expressive tasks helps students develop ideas for argument essays. Using freewriting or idea-mapping, students create a fund of ideas from which they can draw as the course progresses.

Exploration Tasks--Set 2: Exploration and Rehearsal (pp. 73-74)

These eight freewriting tasks help students explore an issue from numerous perspectives. We recommend having students do all eight tasks prior to writing their rough drafts for each formal assignment throughout the course. Among other things, these tasks ask students to search for supporting evidence, to analyze their audiences, to role-play opposing views, and to explore personal experiences relevant to their issues.

Writing Assignments for Chapters 1-3 (pp. 75-77)

Any one of these assignments provides a good initial writing task for the course. The assignments, which assume no knowledge of the text beyond Chapter 3, will enable instructors to assess their students' skills. The assignment options include the following:

a. A self-evaluation letter to the instructor.
b. An argument summary.
c. An analytical essay examining the causes of disagreement between two opposing views.
d. A debate essay written as a mini-play.
e. A letter to the instructor proposing a problem for a major course project.

Writing Assignments for Chapters 4-6 (pp. 138-144)

Designed primarily for freshmen, these short assignments, usually one or two paragraphs long, help students develop specific skills needed for longer arguments. They can be graded rapidly through "models feedback": Rather than placing comments on the papers, the instructor simply assigns a grade after a rapid holistic reading. To provide commentary to students, the instructor duplicates several model performances as well as one or two weaker microthemes. Since all students are writing on the same topic, class discussion of these models can be as instructive as individualized comments. Because the assignments do not require lengthy drafting time on the part of students, we often assign several microthemes a week as we cover Chapters 4-6 in the text. Assignment options are as follows:

   a. Supporting a reason with personal experience data.
   b. Supporting a reason with provided research data.
   c. Supporting a reason by drawing on a newspaper story for data.
   d. Using statistical data to support a point.
   e. A formal argument supporting a claim with several reasons.

Writing Assignments for Chapters 7 and 8 (pp. 187-188)

The first assignment in this group, as well as the last assignment in the group for Chapters 4-6 (Option 5, p. 142), are based on the short form-specified assignments developed by Kenneth Bruffee in A Short Course in Writing, 2nd ed. (Cambridge, Mass.: Winthrop, 1980). The second assignment in this group adapts a similar form-specified approach to Rogerian argument, which we refer to as a conciliatory strategy. The third assignment combines the two or more reasons assignment from Option 5 (p. 142) with the sumnmary and refutation assignment from Option 1 below (p. 187).

   a. A refutation strategy in which the writer summarizes and then refutes an opposing view.
   b. A conciliatory strategy in which the writer summarizes the opposition sympathetically, points out areas of shared values, and presents the writer's compromise position.
   c. A strategy in which the writer adopts the self-announcing structure of the classical argument.

Writing Assignments for Chapters 10-14

Chapters 10-14 in Part Three each includes a writing assignment with accompanying discovery and exploration exercises. The assignments are closely integrated into the content of the chapters so that assigning the writing tasks for each chapter will ensure close reading and study of the text.

Assignment for Chapter 10, "Definition Arguments" (p. 200): The writer is asked to establish criteria for defining a controversial concept such as "cruelty to animals," "true athlete," or "act of courage" and then to argue whether or not a borderline case meets the criteria.

Assignment for Chapter 11, "Causal Arguments" (p. 236): The writer is asked to create an argument identifying "surprising" or "disputed" causes or consequences of a phenomenon.

Assignment for Chapter 12, "Resemblance Arguments" (p. 267): The writer is asked to develop an extended analogy that persuades the audience to accept the writer's view of X. Two alternatives are provided: to develop a precedence argument or to write an analysis of an analogical argument.

Assignment for Chapter 13, "Evaluation Arguments" (p. 283): The writer is asked to evaluate a controversial X such as a controversial rock star, a controversial government policy, or a controversial advertisement.

Assignment for Chapter 14, "Proposal Arguments" (p. 309): The writer is asked to identify a problem, propose a solution, and argue persuasively that the proposal should be adopted. Students are offered several choices: a practical proposal to solve a local problem, an editorial-length proposal argument on a public issue, or a longer formal proposal argument written as a research paper.

Writing Assignments in Part Five (Anthology of Arguments)

The writing assignments in Part Five are "case" assignments designed to engage students in the issues under dispute in the readings. Alternatively, instructors could ask students to write argument analyses of various readings, following the procedures explained in Chapter 2. Instructors will undoubtedly think of many other ways to create writing assignments in response to the readings.

CREATING A SYLLABUS FOR THE COURSE

The text's organization makes it relatively easy to design a course syllabus. Before doing so, however, an instructor needs to make preliminary decisions about the number and kinds of writing assignments to include, about use of class time, and about the amount of textbook material to cover.

Deciding on Writing Assignments for the Course

Instructors have the option of designing their own assignments or using those provided in the text. At the outset instructors should decide how many assignments to include and which ones. We prefer to have a formal assignment due approximately every two weeks, giving us enough class time both for rough draft workshops and for discussion of textbook materials and readings. However, we often assign several microthemes during our discussion of Chapters 4-6._ Here are some typical assignment sequences based on a 16-week semester system:

<u>Sample Assignment Sequence for A Freshman Course</u>
<u>[Excludes Part Three]</u>

- Option 1, p. 75: Letter to teacher about your writing process (due first week)
- "Set 1: Starting Points," pp. 71-73 (to be completed during first two weeks)
- Option 2, p. 76: An argument summary (due second week)
- Option 3, p. 76: An analysis of the sources of disagreement in opposing arguments (due during third week)
- Selected microthemes, Options 1-4, pp. 138-142 (due during fourth and fifth weeks).
- "Set 2: Exploration and Rehearsal," pp. 73-74 (to be completed at the exploration stage for each of the remaining assignments)
- Formal argument using at least two supporting reasons, Option 5, p. 142 (due during sixth week). [NOTE: Some teachers might wish to have the first formal argument due earlier in the term; in such cases, work with Chapters 4-6 can precede work with Chapter 2.]
- Formal argument summarizing and refuting opposition, Option 1, p. 187 (due during eighth week).

- Formal argument using conciliatory strategy, Option 2, p. 188 (due during tenth week)
- An extended argument analysis or position argument based on a set of readings from Part Five [teacher can design the assignment or use one of the "case" assignments from Part Five] (due during the twelfth week)
- A 5-8 page researched argument developed out of the "major course project" initiated from Option 5, p. 77 (due during the sixteenth week)

Alternative Assignment Sequence for a Freshman Course
[Includes Part Three]

- Option 4, p. 76: A debate essay (due at beginning of second week)
- "Set 1: Starting Points," pp. 71-73 (to be completed during first two weeks)
- Option 2, p. 76: An argument summary (due second week)
- Option 3, p. 76: An analysis of the sources of disagreement in opposing arguments (due during third week)
- Selected microthemes, Options 1-5, pp. 138-144 (due during fourth and fifth weeks).
- "Set 2: Exploration and Rehearsal, pp. 73-74 (to be completed at the exploration stage for each of the remaining assignments)
- Option 3, p. 188: A classical argument, p. 188 [combines Option 5, p. 142, and Option 1, p. 187] (due during sixth week)
- Disputed definition assignment from Chapter 10 (due during eighth week)
- Disputed causes or consequence assignment from Chapter 11 (due during tenth week).
- An extended argument analysis or position argument based on a set of readings from Part Five [teacher can design the assignment or use one of the "case" assignments from Part Five] (due during the twelfth week)
- A policy proposal as a research paper from Chapter 14 (due during the sixteenth week)

Sample Assignment Sequence for Advanced Course

- Option 1, p. 75: Letter to teacher about your writing process (due first week)

- "Set 1: Starting Points," pp. 71-73 (to be completed during first two weeks)
- Option 2, p. 76: An argument summary, and Option 3, p. 76: An analysis of the sources of disagreement in opposing arguments (due during second week)
- "Set 2: Exploration and Rehearsal," pp. 73-74 (to be completed at the exploration stage for each of the remaining assignments)
- Option 3, p. 188: A classical argument, p. 188 [combines Option 5, p. 142, and Option 1, p. 187] (due during fourth week)
- Disputed definition assignment from Chapter 10 (due during sixth week)
- Disputed causes or consequence assignment from Chapter 11 (due during eighth week).
- An extended argument analysis or position argument based on a set of readings from Part Five [teacher can design the assignment or use one of the "case" assignments from Part Five] (due during the tenth week).
- An analysis of a resemblance argument from Chapter 12 (due during twelfth week)
- An evaluation argument from Chapter 13 (due during fourteenth week)
- A researched policy proposal from Chapter 14 (due during the sixteenth week)

[Teachers who wish to provide more time between assignments can have students choose either a definition or an evaluation argument--both of which require a criteria-match structure--and either a causal or proposal argument--both of which require causal arguing. An alternative is to require rough drafts of all five of the stasis assignments, but to require revised final products for only two or three of them]

<u>Alternative Assignment Sequence for Advanced Course</u>

Five 3-5-page arguments, two of which address issues of the student's choice and three of which either address issues raised from readings in Part Five or analyze arguments from Part Five. One 7-10-page researched proposal on an issue of public policy.

Using this more open-ended approach, the instructor should tell students that each argument must be addressed toward an actual audience and aimed at publication in a newspaper, magazine, employee bulletin, or newsletter. Since issues of definition, cause, analogy, evaluation, and proposal will naturally occur within students' sequence of six arguments, Part Three of the text will be relevant to these assignments. An essay is due every two weeks from the third through the eleventh weeks. The major proposal argument is due in finished form on the last day of class.

Deciding on Your Use of Class Time

Instructors also need to decide how they wish to use class time--whether in discussion of the rhetoric portions of the text, discussion of readings from Part Five, drafting workshops, collaborative learning tasks, or other group activities such as classroom debates and so forth. We have designed the text to facilitate as much collaborative activity as possible. The <u>For Class Discussion</u> exercises provide small group problem-solving tasks that focus on mastery of text material as well as on discovery and exploration of ideas for arguments.

Deciding on Textbook Materials to Be Covered

Related to one's decision about use of class time is a decision about how much of the text to cover. We believe that students can be asked to read more of a text than is covered in class. In our upper division courses, we spend considerable class time on Part Three of the text. We require students to read and study Parts One and Two with care, but we devote only a few weeks to them, mainly in clarification of enthymemes, the Toulmin analysis schema, and the concepts of <u>logos</u>, <u>ethos</u> and <u>pathos</u>. Freshman students, on the other hand, need to be guided through Parts One and Two rather slowly, so that we often choose to omit much or all of Part Three, especially in a quarter-system freshman course.

As a rule of thumb, we generally ask upper division students to read all of the text, except for those readings in Part Five that we won't be discussing in class or assigning as essay topics. For freshman classes, we often require no more than Chapters 1-8, Appendices One and Two, and selected readings from Part Five, although just as often we try to work in several of the <u>stases</u> chapters from Part Three.

A SAMPLE SYLLABUS FOR A FRESHMAN COURSE USING THE ALTERNATIVE ASSIGNMENT SEQUENCE THAT INCLUDES THE <u>STASES</u> CHAPTERS (PART THREE)

Week One:
--Discussion of Chapter 1 and Appendix 2.
--Planning and drafting of first assignment (Option 4, p. 76, debate essay) which is due at beginning of second week
--Ask students to read Chapters 2 and 3 and assign "Set 1: Starting Points," pp. 71-73 (due at end of second week)
--Begin discussion of Chapter 2.

Week Two:
--Continued discussion of Chapter 2.
--Assign and discuss essays from a topic area in Part Five using the reading/analysis strategies explained in Chapter 2.
--Assign argument summary (Option 2, p. 76), due at end of week
--Students complete "Set 1: Starting Points" (teacher can choose whether to look these over or not).

Week Three:
--Finish discussion of Chapter 2 and selected readings.
--Discussion of Chapter 3
--Assign analysis of sources of disagreement (Option 3, p. 76) for one of the topic areas in Part Five, due at end of the week.

Week Four:
--Discussion of Chapters 4 and 5.
--Assign selected microthemes (Options 1-4, pp. 138-142). [Note: Microthemes are short enough to be completed as overnight homework assignments or they can also be used as in-class collaborative learning tasks.

Week Five:
--Discussion of Chapter 6 and Appendix 1 on logical fallacies.
--Do exercise "Defining Good Argumentative Writing" from end of Appendix Two in order to help establish criteria for arguments.
--Students should begin drafting their essays in response to the assignment "A Classical Argument" (Option 3, p. 188) due at end of seventh week. Prior to drafting, students should explore ideas through exploration tasks, Set 2, pp. 73-74.

Week Six:
--Discussion of Chapters 7 and 8.
--Rough draft workshop for "classical argument."

Week Seven:
--Finish discussion of Chapters 7 and 8.
--Continue draft workshops on classical argument due at end of week.
--Discuss Chapter 9 and assign reading of Chapter 10.

Week Eight:
--Discussion of Chapter 10. [Note: Students should be advised of the last assignment for the semester--a policy argument using research data. At this point in the term, students should begin planning and researching their topics. Ask them to read ahead: Chapter 14 on proposal arguments and Part Four on using the library and the Internet and using sources.]
--Planning and drafting of definitional argument. [Note: The "starling/cruelty to animals" exercise in Chapter 10 is an almost foolproof mind teaser for teaching definitional strategies.]

Week Nine:
--Continued discussion of Chapter 10 including, if desired, professional arguments that turn on definitional issues.
--Revision workshops for definition argument, due end of week.

Weeks Ten and Eleven:
--Discussion of Chapter 10 and associated readings dealing with causal issues.
--Planning, drafting, and revising workshops for causal argument, due at end of week eleven

Weeks Twelve and Thirteen:
--Discussion of essays from one of the topic areas in Part Five. [NOTE: At this point in the semester, students' ability to analyze arguments will be extended and deepened from the experience of studying definitional and causal arguing. Additionally, students' familiarity with Toulmin's system and with the concepts of logos, ethos, and pathos will enable students to evaluate arguments with greater confidence and subtlety than they exhibited early in the term.]

--Draft workshops for essay due at the end of week thirteen, based on the readings. This can be either the "case" assignment provided in the text or an analytical assignment designed by the teacher.

Weeks Fourteen, Fifteen, and Sixteen:
--Discussion of Chapter 14 on proposal arguments and of Chapter 17 on use of sources.
--Planning and drafting of researched proposal argument due last day of term.
--Revision workshops for proposal argument.

HOW THIS TEXT TREATS "INVENTION"

Much of this text focuses on the invention of arguments. The core of invention, for us, is the enthymeme, a concept that urges students to seek supporting reasons that are rooted in assumptions shared by the audience. We thus spend considerable class time with the collaborative tasks in Chapters 4-9 helping students understand "because clauses" as enthymemes with unstated assumptions. Using Toulmin's schema, students can flesh out their "because clauses" by seeking grounds that support the stated reasons and by seeking backing to support the often unstated warrants, all the while remaining aware of opposing views (conditions for rebuttal, qualifiers). Our whole treatment of the Toulmin schema for the expansion of arguments is thus a part of invention. Additional approaches to invention, including use of the stock issues and the "three steps" strategy (arguing from principle, from consequences, and from analogy) are introduced to students in Part Three. Finally, "Set 2: Exploration and Rehearsal" (pp. 73-74) uses freewriting and idea-mapping to encourage exploratory thinking about an argument prior to composing the first draft. We recommend that students do the eight tasks in this sequence for each of their formal essays in the course.

USING <u>FOR CLASS DISCUSSION</u> EXERCISES AS COLLABORATIVE LEARNING TASKS

Although the <u>For Class Discussion</u> exercises work well as stimuli for conventional class discussions, they have been designed especially as collaborative tasks. In our own approach to using the exercises, we divide the class into small groups, asking each group to work independently on the tasks prior to a concluding plenary session in which groups' solutions are compared and debated. In our conduct of collaborative tasks, we have been influenced by Kenneth Bruffee's work on collaborative learning, by George Hillock's description of the "environmental mode" of teaching, and by Harvey Wiener's discussion of assessment of collaborative learning (see bibliography at the end of this Instructor's Manual).

Design of Collaborative Tasks
Well-designed collaborative tasks should meet the following criteria: (1) Tasks should ask groups to produce something that the group recorder or leader presents to the whole class during the plenary session at the end. This "something" could be a thesis sentence, a brief paragraph, a tree diagram, an idea-map, and so forth. By making groups responsible for a product, the teacher insures that groups stay on task. Tasks that simply ask groups to "discuss" something often lead to diffuse, unproductive sessions. (2) Tasks should focus on learning objectives for the course, and students should be able to see the purpose of the task in terms of course design. (3) The task should be manageable within a set time period. Generally, we recommend tasks that take 15-30 minutes to accomplish so that students shuttle back and forth between small group work and plenary work led by the instructor. (4) The task should be put in writing (often on an overhead projector) and should specify clearly what the students are to do. (5) A time limit should be placed on the board (for example, "Report in 20 minutes" or "Report at 1:50"). The For Class Discussion exercises in the text meet all these criteria except for the last: the teacher needs to determine how much class time to devote to the task before moving to the plenary sessions.

Dividing the Class into Collaborative Groups
Teachers often ask about ways to divide students into groups. Some teachers try to arrange groups to maximize diversity--good writers placed with weak writers, men placed with women, engineers placed with art majors, and so forth. Our own experience suggests that randomly arranged groups work about as well as carefully designed groups and save the

instructor considerable time. Our own procedure is to divide the class randomly into groups of five. We do, however, try to keep an even mix of men and women in each group.

Forming Collaborative Groups that Can Also Meet Outside of Class As Study Groups or Revision Teams

Sometimes instructors want their collaborative groups to meet together outside of class--a constraint that can lead to scheduling headaches since random groups will invariably include people with conflicting class and work schedules. For a solution, try the following. Tell all people who have a free hour between 8:00 a.m. and 10:00 a.m. to meet in one corner of the room. Then in another corner assemble people who have a free hour from 10:00 to 12:00, then 12:00 to 2:00 and so forth throughout the day and evening. Finally, group those with a free hour on Saturdays or Sundays. Give the groups fifteen minutes to work out schedules among themselves. Tell them that there must be at least three people to a group and no more than five.

Should Groups Stay Together All Term or Should Groups Be Switched As the Term Progresses?

In our opinion, there is no right answer to this question; the advantages and disadvantages of each procedure balance out. Our own tendency is to keep the same groups together all term unless we have a dysfunctional group, but many of our colleagues prefer moving groups around to stimulate freshness and expose persons to as many different points of view as possible.

What About Non-Native Speakers?

Collaborative learning is an excellent teaching method for non-native speakers of English. We recommend that second-language students be mixed randomly within the collaborative groups. We encourage groups to discover issues that take advantage of cross-cultural differences. Some of the best argumentative essays in our classes have grown out of multi-cultural groups ("Should corporal punishment be used as a motivating device for students?"--one of our Malaysian students argued that being caned in front of class is a wonderfully motivating procedure; "Are arranged marriages more successful than romantic marriages?"--an Indian student argued for the advantages of arranged marriages).

Instructor's Role During the Collaborative Task

There is much disagreement here. Ken Bruffee advises teachers to leave the room during the collaborative task and to return only for the plenary session. Other teachers like to move quietly from group to group listening in on the sessions and being available to answer questions. (Bruffee argues that a teacher "listening in" changes the dynamic of the group.) Still others like to join a group as a fellow discussant, encouraging students to regard the instructor as just another student. This method can work well if an instructor is able to overcome his or her privileged status. Using this method, the instructor joins a different group each time. Our own method is to leave the room for the first five or ten minutes of a task in order to free up the discussions. Then we sit quietly in different parts of the room, listening in on different groups without appearing to join them.

Instructor's Role During the Plenary Session

Here is where instructors earn their combat pay. After collaborative tasks, when students have arrived at their own points of view and are emboldened by consensus of their groups, they can become passionate presenters of their positions. When disagreement occurs between groups, teachers can ask group recorders to debate the issue or can simply use the disagreement to initiate general class discussion.

The most sensitive moments occur when the class reaches a consensus solution different from the instructor's. The collaborative classroom posits a world view in which the instructor is not the sole source of knowledge or authority. The instructor cannot therefore rely on "authority" to give a privileged status to his or her solution. Rather, the instructor must argue his or her case reasonably, just as the students must argue theirs, and hope that the reasonableness of the presentation wins the day. These moments, for us, provide the ideal learning environment for a class devoted to argument.

USING COLLABORATIVE GROUPS FOR WRITING PROCESS WORKSHOPS

The <u>For Class Discussion</u> exercises are aimed primarily at helping collaborative groups become engaged with the subject matter of the text. As such, they are mainly content-centered exercises.

However, collaborative groups can also be used successfully for workshops on rough drafts and on other phases of the writing process. Appendix Two gives numerous suggestions for using groups to help with writing. What follows are some further suggestions.

Using Collaborative Groups for Invention and Exploration

Early in the term, we recommend using the collaborative tasks in Chapter 3 to encourage students to participate in argumentative discussions. These tasks will help students discover issues that both interest them and engage controversy.

Once a writer has chosen an issue, groups are especially effective at encouraging exploration. Working either in groups of five or of three or two, students can be asked to share each other's issues and brainstorm reasons for and against each other's preliminary claims.

Once a writer has selected an issue, arrived at a preliminary claim, and explored ideas through group work and through doing "Set 2--Exploration and Rehearsal" (pp. 73-74), they can be placed in pairs and asked to interview each other about the planned argument. Each writer should "talk through" the argument with the listener, rehearsing ideas orally before writing a draft.

Using Collaborative Groups for Revision

We ask writers to bring legible copies of complete drafts to a rough draft workshop. There are several ways that rough draft workshops can be handled.

In Class Workshops

In class workshops can be effective in group sizes from pairs to five persons (although five people often don't have enough time to respond to each person's draft in a 50-minute period). We ask students either to exchange drafts in the group or between groups. (When drafts are exchanged between groups, group members can collaborate on responses without the writer's being present--a factor that often encourages more detailed and more frank criticism.) We generally ask students to follow a specific checksheet that we pass out in advance. Occasionally, we ask critiquers to make paragraph-by-paragraph "says" and "does" statements for the writer's essay and/or a written summary of the writer's argument. If critiquers have trouble doing so, then the remainder of the session can focus on problems of clarity in the draft, with critiquers explaining to the writer where the confusion occurs. Once the argument is reasonably clear, comments can focus on the rhetorical concerns highlighted in the checksheet.

At home critiques

Some instructors prefer having students critique each other's work outside of class. One way to do so is to have students make two copies of their drafts. In class, divide students into pairs who will work together as critiquing teams. Students A and B exchange drafts with students C and D. Outside of class, students A and B meet to critique C's and D's drafts while C and D meet to critique drafts from A and B. Each pair collaborates to write out a detailed critique of the two drafts. In class, the pairs meet to share their critiques of each other's drafts.

A variation on this procedure, which permits students more time to devote to the process (and subsequently to reflect on and learn from it), is to have students on the day that drafts are due bring to class enough copies of their drafts for all the members of their workshop group (plus one for the instructor), exchange their copies with those of the other members of their workshop group, and then perform the critiques of those drafts individually outside of class according to a checklist that the instructor provides. Students return the next class period to share their critiques with the writers in the context of their workshop group. This method also has the virtue of permitting a "dry run" of the review procedure, for on the day drafts are due, once the initial exchange of drafts has been accomplished, the instructor may spend the remaining class time leading students in an application of the checklist to a sample student or professional essay, thereby modelling for the students the procedure they are to follow in performing their own critiques. At the conclusion of the following class period, once students have had the opportunity to share their critiques with one another and once the instructor has had the opportunity to (at least) skim all of the drafts, the instructor may take a few moments both to solicit from the students the major problems they encountered in their peers' responses to the assignment and to point out any problems he or she noticed to be common to many of the drafts. The class may then be engaged in a discussion of possible solutions to those problems.

Regardless of the peer review strategy instructors choose to use, we recommend that instructors take the time to review at least one set of the drafts written in response to each major assignment, however briefly, before the final version is due. Skimming a set of drafts affords an instructor the opportunity to discover if a particular student or a whole class of students has missed the boat on an assignment in time to intervene at a productive point in the process and so encourage individual conferences or design more extensive, full class explanations. To ensure that the instructor's response to the drafts does not threaten to supersede the more detailed, draft-specific critiques provided by the other students, we prefer not to comment specifically on each draft but rather to conclude the class period in which students share their critiques with one another with our own generic critique of students' response to the assignment.

Using Collaborative Groups for Editing

Pairs work best here. Students bring late-stage drafts to class and exchange them in pairs. Students are responsible for helping each other edit for sentence errors. Sometimes teachers can hold the editor--as opposed to the writer--responsible for certain kinds of errors in the writer's draft, operating on the principle that it is often easier to spot errors in someone else's essay than in your own.

SUGGESTIONS FOR TEACHING THE TOULMIN SYSTEM

Although Toulmin's system of argument analysis is widely discussed in the pedagogical literature and used regularly in argument textbooks, no two sources discuss it in exactly the same way, and most instructors, if honest, would confess to difficulties in teaching it. Moreover, teachers familiar with Toulmin's own work may be puzzled by the way we have superimposed the language of enthymemes (a claim with a stated reason and a missing premise) on Toulmin's language of grounds, warrants, and backing. For these reasons, instructors using <u>Writing Arguments</u> might find it useful to know why and how we have adapted Toulmin to our purposes as well as to see how we teach Toulmin to students in argument courses.

How and Why We Have Added Enthymemic Language to Toulmin's System

Instructors familiar with Toulmin's pioneering work <u>The Uses of Argument</u> [Cambridge University Press: Cambridge, 1958] will recall that in Toulmin's system the arguer begins with a conviction about factual data, the "Grounds" that Toulmin calls "what we have to go on." The arguer moves directly from the Grounds to the Claim by means of the coordinate conjunction "so" or the conjunctive adverb "therefore." His seminal example concerns a certain Harry, born in Bermuda.

Harry was born in Bermuda, so Harry is a British subject.

To analyze the underlying logic of this statement, Toulmin develops a complete system, which he diagrams as follows (<u>Uses of Argument</u>, p. 105):

[BACKING]
On account of the following statutes and legal provisions:
|
|
[WARRANT]
Since a man born in Bermuda will generally be a British subject.
|
|
[GROUNDS]   [QUALIFIER]   [CLAIM]
Harry was born in Bermuda ➡ so [presumably]   Harry is a
                                                     | British subject.
                                                     |
[CONDITIONS OF REBUTTAL]
unless both his parents were aliens/
unless he has become a naturalized American citizen/
etc. . . .

Toulmin's intention here is not to write a textbook on argument but to enter a philosophic discourse on the way humans establish conviction about claims. His concern is to show the limits of formal logic for real language arguments--in his terms to "reject as confused a conception of 'deductive inference' which many recent philosophers have accepted without hesitation as impeccable" (Preface)--and to propose an alternative approach adapted from legal disputation. Despite the success and importance of his work, from the standpoint of teaching argument to college students, we find three difficulties with Toulmin's original system.

First, Toulmin's approach often seems curiously non-rhetorical. In the case of Harry from Bermuda, for example, we are apparently to presume that there is some sort of dispute going on about Harry's citizenship, but Toulmin never tells us who is disputing Harry's citizenship under what circumstances, as if a question at issue is irrelevant. Without some larger question at issue, however, we would have no clue about the contextual meaning of the grounds, which could support an infinite number of different claims:

> Harry was born in Bermuda, so he likes to scuba dive.
> Harry was born in Bermuda, so he should adopt to the Florida climate better than Yukon Bob.
> Harry was born in Bermuda, so you should interview him rather than Yukon Bob for your report on British colonialism.

It is clear that data by themselves are inert until they are related contextually to some meaning-creating assertion. In argumentation, these assertions arise out of different points of view related to a question at issue. By starting with the grounds rather than with the issue, Toulmin has no language for discussing the rhetorical conversation out of which disputes arise. This is no weakness for Toulmin himself, whose interests are epistemological rather than rhetorical, but it poses a substantial problem to teachers of argument.

Related to the first problem is a second one. Toulmin's system provides no slots for the common language terms "reason" and "because." These are such familiar, useful, and powerful terms (What is your <u>reason</u> for believing X? Well, <u>because</u> . . .) that it seemed unwise to us to adopt a system of argument analysis that had no place for them. Toulmin couldn't use these terms precisely because he starts with the data [Grounds] rather than with an issue and competing claims. By starting with data he is committed to a "Grounds, therefore Claim" structure rather than a "Claim because Reason" structure.

A third problem with Toulmin's system is that Toulmin seems to have a positivist faith in the factualness of facts. His system therefore has difficulty describing arguments in which the "facts of the case" are at issue. For Toulmin, Grounds are hard data, the indisputable facts ("what we have to go on") from which we make the inductive leap to our claim. If the facts are in dispute, then they aren't facts, and we have nothing to go on. But real world arguments often start in uncertainty about the facts, and we need a system that allows us to examine that uncertainty. Suppose, for example, that we have a real dispute about Harry's citizenship--that we are detectives, say, working on a case that turns on Harry's citizenship.

> "Why do you think Harry is a British subject?" I ask you.
> "Because he was born in Bermuda," you reply.
> "Why do you think he was born in Bermuda?"
> "His mother told me so, and besides, I have seen his birth certificate."

In this conversation, Toulmin's original hard datum (Harry was born in Bermuda) shifts its status from "fact" to proposition. It is now a new claim supported by a lower order of facts--his mother's testimony and a birth certificate. So when is a fact a fact?

As one looks through the examples in Toulmin's <u>Uses of Argument</u>, one senses his uneasiness with any argument in which the facts of the case are in doubt. Until you establish the facts, he explains, you have no grounds for argument. His belief that arguments can be grounded in correct facts leads to an unexamined inconsistency in his discussions of data throughout his book. Sometimes the grounds in his examples are indeed hard facts--physically verifiable data--but at other times his grounds are higher order claims summarizing the meaning he finds in the data, claims that seem to us very much like reasons. (Perhaps Toulmin doesn't distinguish between grounds and reason because he sees a generalization about the meaning of data as a non-problematic, correct summary of the facts rather than an interpretive claim.) Thus to us "Harry was born in Bermuda" is certainly a plausible reason for believing Harry is a British subject, but it may or may not be a fact. Consider, then, the difference between Toulmin's original casting of Harry's case and our own casting of it as follows:

Issue: Is Harry a British subject?
Enthymeme: Harry is a British subject because he was born in Bermuda.
Claim: Harry is a British subject.
Stated reason: because he was born in Bermuda.
Grounds: evidence that he was born in Bermuda (mother's testimony, birth certificate, etc.)
Warrant: People born in Bermuda will generally be British subjects.
Backing: The following national and international laws and statutes:
Qualifier: presumably, probably
Conditions of rebuttal: (attacking grounds and stated reason): unless his mother is lying and his birth records forged; (attacking warrant and backing): unless both his parents were aliens, unless he has renounced his citizenship and is a naturalized citizen elsewhere)

As can be seen, in adapting Toulmin we start with the enthymeme rather than with the grounds. We begin with the enthymeme because, for us, it is the single most powerful teaching tool that we know in helping college students understand argument. Unlike inert data, the enthymeme is a contextual, rhetorical concept that depends on a question at issue (and hence an audience), a claim, a reason, and an unstated premise that necessitates attention to the audience's values. [An excellent introduction to the concept of enthymeme--one that has proven formative for us--is John T. Gage's "Teaching the Enthymeme: Invention and Arrangement" in <u>Rhetoric Review</u>, 2 (September 1983), 38-50]. Moreover, the enthymeme can be quickly taught to students in familiar ordinary language as a claim supported by a reason expressed as a because clause.

In our own teaching of argument, the concept of the enthymeme takes precedence over Toulmin. In fact, one can use Writing Arguments with only minimal attention to Toulmin, but the concept of the enthymeme (claim, reason, unstated assumption) is crucial. However, Toulmin's system meshes easily with the enthymeme--so easily, in fact, that we prefer to think of our marriage of the enthymeme and Toulmin's system as a refinement or improvement of Toulmin rather than a modification or departure. Toulmin's Grounds now become the facts and evidence used to support the Stated Reason in the enthymeme; the Warrant, as in Toulmin, is the unstated assumption linking the reason and grounds to the Claim; the Backing supports the Warrant, and the Conditions of Rebuttal expose the conditions under which the claim will not hold because either the facts of the case can be questioned or because the warrant can be questioned.

Why We Use Toulmin: The Evolution of Our Approach to Argument

Instructors might better appreciate the value of Toulmin analysis if they know the reasons that we adopted it and particularly the kinds of writing problems that Toulmin's analysis helped us solve.

Our approach to teaching composition changed substantially in the early 1980s when Professor Kenneth Bruffee of Brooklyn College gave a workshop at Montana State University where we were then colleagues together. Bruffee, as the profession's chief proponent and apologist for collaborative learning, introduced us to the use of small groups in the classroom and inspired the emphasis on collaborative learning throughout Writing Arguments.

For several years at Montana State University, we also adopted Bruffee's textbook A Short Course in Writing, which took a form-prescribed (some might say "by the numbers") approach to the teaching of argument through a sequence of three-paragraph essays:

Two Reasons:
    paragraph 1: Introduction to issue followed by claim
    paragraph 2: First supporting reason with development
    paragraph 3: Second supporting reason with development

Nestorian Order:
>   paragraph 1: Introduction to issue followed by claim
>   paragraph 2: Summary of several less important reasons
>   paragraph 3: Major supporting reason with development

Strawman:
>   paragraph 1: Introduction to issue followed by claim
>   paragraph 2: Summary of opposing view
>   paragraph 3: Refutation of opposing view

Concession:
>   paragraph 1: Introduction to issue followed by claim
>   paragraph 2: Summary of opposing view
>   paragraph 3: Concession to opposing view followed by own argument

The influence of Bruffee's assignment sequence is still evident in Part Two of Writing Arguments, where our "supporting reasons," "opposition/refutation," and "Conciliatory/Rogerian" assignments are all adaptations of Bruffee's prescribed-form approach. Moreover, Bruffee's influence can also be felt in the tendency of all our student example essays to have the highly structured, top-down, "boxy" shape that results from a teaching approach that sacrifices stylistic and rhetorical sophistication for the conceptual and cognitive clarity that highly structured forms require and promote.

Although we were pleased with the argumentative focus that the Bruffee assignments produced, student essays tended to be disappointingly thin. In the early days of our teaching of argument, we had no consistent strategy for teaching students to generate and analyze arguments. We tried to supplement Bruffee with instruction on informal fallacies and syllogistic logic, but we found that these approaches had almost no generative benefit and didn't produce the kinds of productive classroom discussion that led to more detailed and elaborated arguments.

The solution for us became our integration of the enthymeme and Toulmin's system. We saw almost immediate improvement in the quality of our students' papers in terms of increased elaboration and development, heightened sense of audience, and willingness to examine underlying assumptions.

A Classroom Strategy for Teaching Toulmin

All that remained for us was the development of an effective pedagogical strategy for introducing Toulmin to students in a way that makes them see Toulmin's power without intimidating them. The strategy we use is to begin with plenty of clearcut, easy examples. The <u>For Class Discussion</u> exercises in Chapters 4 and 5 are particularly helpful in this regard.

The central feature of our pedagogy is to begin with the enthymeme rather than with Toulmin and to get students used to the enthymemic concepts of issue, claim, stated reason, and unstated assumption before introducing Toulmin language. On the day that we assign students to read Chapters 4 and 5, we put the following enthymemes on an overhead.

Issue: What car should we buy?
Enthymeme 1: We should buy this Geo Metro because it is extremely economical.
Enthymeme 2: We should buy this used Volvo because it is very safe.
Enthymeme 3: We should buy this Ford Falcon because it is red.

Our hope is that students will find something humorously fishy about Enthymeme 3 as soon as they see it, even if they can't yet quite articulate what's wrong with it. Before getting specifically to Enthymeme 3, however, we conduct a general class discussion about each of the enthymemes. We begin by getting students to articulate the unstated assumption behind each enthymeme.

Assumption for Enthymeme 1: We should buy the car that is most economical. (Economy is the major criterion we should use in selecting a car.)
Assumption for Enthymeme 2: We should buy the car that is most safe. (Safety is the major criterion we should use in selecting a car.)
Assumption for Enthymeme 3: We should buy a car that is red. (The color red is the major criterion we should use in selecting a car.)

We then enter a general discussion of Enthymemes 1 and 2 by talking about how we would support them or try to refute them. One possibility is that we might agree with the criterion in Enthymemes 1 and 2 but disagree with the stated reason by arguing that the Geo Metro isn't as economical as another car or that the Volvo isn't as safe as another car. But another possibility is that we might disagree with the criterion in each case and thus argue that we should base our decision not on economy or safety but on performance or driving fun or cargo space or reliability. The key here is to have students see the difference between supporting or attacking the stated reason itself versus supporting or attacking the unstated assumption behind the reason.

We then switch to Enthymeme 3 and ask students why they thought something was fishy about that enthymeme. We say tongue in cheek that we see nothing wrong with it. We assure them that the reason is a really true--we can verify that the car is red through both the testimony of a survey of randomly chosen people (100 percent said the car was red) and through a special chemical spectroscopy test we ran on the paint. "No," they will say. "That's not what's at issue. We agree that the car's red, but we can't see what color has to do with buying the car." Then we'll reply, "Oh, you can't see how we get from the facts to the claim" (echoing Toulmin's phrase that the warrant is how you get from data to claim). Or, "So you think the claim is un<u>warrant</u>ed?" (trying to work in some Toulmin language naturally). "What we need, then, is some kind of argument to '<u>back</u> up' this unstated assumption that redness is the major criterion we should choose."

At this point, we begin introducing Toulmin terminology to students. The unstated assumption behind each enthymeme we now call the warrant. Together the claim, the stated reason, and the warrant constitute the frame or skeleton of the argument. These frame sentences can be stated in a single sentence each:

Claim: We should buy this used Volvo.
Stated Reason: It is very safe.
Warrant: We should buy the car that is the safest.

We explain that what fleshes out the argument--what gives it development and detail--are the grounds and/or the backing.

The grounds, we say, are all the facts, data, examples, evidence, or chains of reasons we use to support the stated reason. The backing is all the facts, data, evidence, examples, or chains of reasons we use to support the warrant. Whether we concentrate on providing grounds, backing, or both depends on where we anticipate our audience's needs and objections.

We now go back to discuss each enthymeme again, this time using Toulmin terminology. We take the class through a series of questions like these:

1. Imagine a situation in which a writer might need to provide extensive grounds for Enthymeme 1, but no backing. What would that situation be? What kinds of grounds might you use? [Possible answer: Writer and audience have already agreed that economy is the chief criterion for choosing the car; they are disagreeing on which of two cars is the most economical. The writer supporting the Geo Metro might provide grounds in the form of data about fuel economy, maintenance costs, taxes and licensing fees, and resale value.]

2. Imagine a situation in which a writer might need to provide backing for Enthymeme 2, but no grounds. What would that situation be? What kind of argument could be devised for backing? [Possible answer: Writer and audience agree that Volvos are very safe, but they disagree on whether safety should be the primary criterion. The writer might argue that this car is for a very safety-minded middle class couple with young children. The husband of the couple lost a sister in an auto accident several years ago and is obsessed with safety. He could never enjoy driving or riding in a car that wasn't, in his mind, the safest car he could buy. The wife of the couple has similar concerns for safety.]

3. Now reverse the situation and imagine a scenario that requires no backing for Enthymeme 2, but plenty of grounds. [Here writer and audience have agreed that they will buy the safest car on the market, but there is disagreement over whether a used Volvo is the safest car. To argue for the Volvo's safety, the writer might provide grounds in the form of insurance claim data, crash test data, data about the actual construction of the car, and so forth.]

Finally, we move to a discussion of Enthymeme 3. We ask why something seemed fishy about that enthymeme from the start. The answer, which can now be cast in Toulmin terms, is that the Warrant seems silly. We can readily see how economy or safety could be a criterion for buying a car, but not redness. In Toulmin's term, this enthymeme cries out for backing:

> **Claim:** We should buy this Ford Falcon.
> **Stated Reason:** It is red.
> **Grounds:** Direct observation; 100 percent consensus on informal survey that the car is red; statement "red" under "color" on sales form; scientific analysis of light spectrum as it is reflected from car's surface.
> **Warrant:** If we find a car that's red, we should buy it.
> **Backing:** ? ? ?

We then ask students either individually or in small groups to think of some kind of scenario in which one really might buy a car because it is red. In short, we ask them to think of a way to provide backing for the warrant. After students share some of their ideas, we put the following argument on the overhead [which is a true case--John Bean's neighbor in the Ford Falcon era bought a little red Falcon for his mother for exactly the reasons stated]:

> You must think it ludicrous that I think we should buy the Falcon because it is red. But think for a minute about Grandma's situation. Grandpa died four months ago. Grandma has hardly left the house since then and needs to snap out of her depression. She likes to drive, even though Grandpa usually did all the driving in that clunky old Buick they owned. She never liked that car, and she won't drive it now--maybe because it reminds her of Grandpa. What Grandma needs is a sporty, new, little, easy-to-drive-and-park car. So, of course, redness isn't the only criteria we should think about. But there are dozens of sporty little cars on the market that fit our other criteria. What is most important, I think, is that the car be red. That has always been her favorite color. It is youthful and energetic. I think a little red car will help her snap out of her mourning and get her out of the house. And let's get it for her by next Monday, her birthday. Let's have her wake

up and see her own little red car in the driveway. So I say, let's go get the Falcon. It's available today, and it is just exactly the kind of red that will perk Grandma up.

These what-car-should-we-buy examples have proven effective for us in teaching students the difference between grounds and backing. Clearly, to provide grounds for Enthymeme 3 would be comically pointless. Nobody disputes the car's color in the way they might dispute the car's economy or safety. Just as clearly, it is essential to provide backing for Enthymeme 3 because no one will accept redness as a plausible criterion for buying a car the way they might accept economy or safety. The obvious difference between grounds and backing in Enthymeme 3 helps students see the distinction between grounds and backing in the other arguments also. Likewise, they see how Toulmin's system helps them make rhetorical decisions: Will my audience accept my stated reason? If not, I need substantial grounds. Will they accept my warrant? If not, I will need to make it explicit and provide backing.

Once students feel comfortable using the Toulmin language to determine and analyze strategies of support for the what-car-should-we-buy enthymemes, they are prepared to read Chapters 4 and 5 and to do the For Class Discussion exercises, where their understanding of the concepts can be strengthened and deepened.

What About Messy Student Examples of Enthymemes that Don't "Fit" Toulmin's Schema?

Of course, doing these exercises on textbook examples, where the enthymemes have been selected because the distinctions between stated reason and warrant and between grounds and backing are especially clear, won't mean that all enthymemes are equally easy to analyze. In the heat of real-world arguments students often produce enthymemes that baffle us with their complexity. Sometimes the grammar is tangled; sometimes several lines of argument are conflated; sometimes important intermediate steps are omitted; sometimes the enthymeme seems like a hopeless non sequitur; sometimes the argument seems OK but we just can't quite unravel its parts in Toulmin's terms.

Therefore, after doing the For Class Discussion exercises in Chapters 4 and 5, all of which are analyzable using Toulmin's schema, we like to give students a taste of a non-textbook example of an enthymeme that is more like the ones they are apt to produce or encounter. A typical example is the following, which we put on an overhead.

> We need to start a women's studies program at Clambake College because women are sick and tired of being treated as unequals.

Most of our students think this is a good argument until we begin trying to analyze it in Toulmin's terms. We look first at the stated reason

> Women are sick and tired of being treated as unequals.

and ask how we might support it with grounds. Would we provide evidence that women are "sick and tired" (examples of frustrated women--narratives, say, of women faculty or students who are near points of exhaustion?) or evidence that women have been treated as unequals (data, say, about unequal pay or about the glass ceiling)? When we ask questions like these, students begin seeing that the reason has two parts that aren't clearly connected. The reason, as stated, doesn't help us know what kind of evidence to provide.

We encounter more confusion when we try to articulate the warrant. When asked to write out what they think is the warrant, many students will be unable to do so (this example doesn't click the way the textbook examples do). Those who try will disagree on how to word it. (We ourselves can't write a warrant for this enthymeme, other than an unsatisfactory if-then statement: "If something causes women to be sick and tired at being treated as unequals, then we should start a women's studies program" [?]) We make more progress by asking the simpler question, "What are some of the unstated assumptions behind this enthymeme?" It is easy to see some: It is bad to feel sick and tired; it is bad to be treated as unequals. But what, we ask, do these bad things have to do with a women's studies program? Perhaps students will say, "A women's studies program will help end or eliminate these bad things"--an insightful answer that moves us forward.

At this point we try to show that one problem with the original enthymeme is that it contains no term shared by both the claim and the stated reason. In other words the stated reason doesn't repeat a key term from the claim. The claim is about starting a women's studies program, while the stated reason is about women's being sick and tired at being treated as unequals. Because the term "women's studies program" or "starting a women's studies program" doesn't appear in the stated reason, it is difficult to write a warrant that connects stated reason to claim. We ask students to revise the original enthymeme in order to repeat in the stated reason this key term from the claim.

> We should start a women's studies program because doing so [e.g. starting a women's studies program] will...
>
> We should start a women's studies program because it [e.g. a women's studies program] will...

Students can now break down the original bifurcated reason into its constituent parts:

> We should start a women's studies program because such a program will help promote equality of women and men in our society. [Develops the "treated as unequals" part of the original enthymeme]
>
> We should start a women's studies program here at Clambake College because doing so will help end the frustration and powerlessness felt by many women students and faculty who have spent years battling a patriarchal administration. [Develops the "women are sick and tired" part of the original enthymeme]

Once the enthymemes are worded this way, they become more readily analyzable in Toulmin's terms. Students agree that it is easier to see how to develop each of these enthymemes than was the case with the original enthymeme. This exercise helps students see that it can be worthwhile sometimes to examine their own enthymemes from a Toulmin perspective. Trying to analyze them in Toulmin's terms can be a salutary exercise in clarifying the lines of reasoning to be developed. But we don't insist that students master Toulmin. Like other heuristics, the Toulmin system is not an end in itself but only a means to better structured and developed arguments. It is the quality of writing that we are most interested in.

II. SUGGESTED ANSWERS TO FOR CLASS DISCUSSION EXERCISES

Chapter 1

(p. 6) 1) As the text explains, explicit arguments state their claims directly and work to support those claims with reasons and evidence. Thus does the first paragraph announce its claim in the first sentence: colleges should abolish cheerleaders in order to reduce the perpetuation of sexual stereotypes. The remaining sentences all serve to provide evidence in support of that claim. While the second paragraph also makes an argument of sorts, it is one that a reader has to infer from what is said--the writer's persuasive purpose is by no means obvious. 2) A variation of this exercise is to ask students to bring to class examples of advertisements that represent implicit arguments in order to discuss the persuasive strategies they employ and the ways advertisers guide readers in how to interpret and respond to them.

(pp. 15-17) The purpose of this exercise is to stimulate class discussion and reveal to students the complexity of issues that turn on differences of values and belief. The teacher can either lead a general class discussion on the value conflicts in these newspapers stories or conduct simulation games as suggested in the task itself. The easiest way to run the simulation game is first to assign students into small groups, with each group assigned to one of the roles. Ask the groups to brainstorm all the arguments the assigned "role" is apt to make. Then each group can select a spokesperson to play the role in the actual simulation. Here are examples of the kinds of arguments that should emerge from the simulation:
 Caesarian section case: The mother's attorney should argue for the rights of the mother, for freedom of religion, and the right of privacy of the individual from being forced to undergo an operation against her will. Analogies might be made to the

"consent forms" that all patients now sign when undergoing medical procedures. These imply not only that the state can't force you to have an operation but that doctors can't require an operation without your full consent. The attorney representing the fetus should argue for the right of the unborn person to a healthy life. Not only does the mother's refusal threaten the fetus's life, but it also threatens possible permanent mental retardation. The mother's religious beliefs can't be allowed to threaten another person's life or subject person to lifelong retardation. Analogies might be made to cases where freedom of religion have been abridged to protect others (animal sacrifice, severe disciplining of children, withholding of medical care from children, etc.). Other relevant arguments might include the financial cost to the state of caring for a retarded infant, the general sense in the United States of the superiority of science over spiritualism in treatment of disease, and so forth.

Crossburning case: This is a particularly troublesome issue, for it pits the value of free speech against the value of eliminating racism and prejudice. Supporters of the right to burn crosses will need to argue that even the most hateful kind of free speech (including openly racist speech on campuses?) is constitutionally protected and that cross burning is a symbolic form of speech. Opponents of cross burning will need to argue that (a) there are limits to free speech if it harms other people and/or that (b) cross burning isn't "speech" in the constitutional terms.

Panhandling ban: This case is a good introduction to the anthology unit on "Social Policy Toward the Homeless Mentally Ill"--a topic also developed in Charles Krauthammer's argument in Chapter 10 and student writer Stephen Bean's counter-argument in Chapter 14. This case pits the rights of homeless people to use public property versus the rights of shoppers and business people to have a clean and pleasant downtown city. Supporters of the homeless should argue that sitting is not a crime, that the economy doesn't provide adequate housing, jobs, or medical care for poor people, that no public restrooms are available, and that asking for money is legal (what is the difference between a homeless person asking for money and a Salvation Army person ringing a bell at Christmas?, someone might ask). Supporters of a vibrant downtown should argue that panhandlers hurt business, that the foul smell of urine and feces drives away shoppers, that the deterioration of downtown businesses harms the city's economy making it impossible to provide the services that homeless people need, that enforcement of these laws will force at least some of the homeless to seek treatment for chemical dependency and begin turning their lives around, and so forth.

(p. 22) In our experience, almost all students vote to approve Gordon Adams' petition, thus waiving his math requirement. The text takes up the Gordon Adams' case again in Chapter 7 in the section on audience-based reasons (pp. 147-148). For the present exercise, it is useful for the instructor to help students see the issue from the faculty's perspective. Would faculty accept Gordon's basic assumption that career utility is the prime consideration for requiring a core course? Would granting Gordon's petition set a precedent for waiving any core course that is irrelevant to a student's chosen career? For this exercise, also help students observe metacognitively their own decision-making processes. Ask for examples of how students' ideas evolved during the discussion. We like to praise students who admit changing their position as a result of listening to good arguments from fellow students.

Chapter 2

(p. 34) **Paragraph 13:** <u>Does</u>: Begins to introduce solution to illegitimacy by outlining dynamics of cultural restraints. <u>Says</u>: Adolescent boys desire sex and young girls desire babies; therefore societies have erected social constraints to channel these desires into marriage.
    Paragraph 14: <u>Does</u>: Defines the underlying ethical premise of his proposal. <u>Says</u>: "The child deserves society's support. The parent does not."
    Paragraph 15: <u>Does</u>: Defines the underlying social justification for his proposal. <u>Says</u>: Because the American way of life values legal freedoms, we must depend on non-governmental constraints to curb illegitimacy.
    Paragraph 16: <u>Does</u>: justifies his proposal to those who might think of it as social engineering. <u>Says</u>: His proposal is not social engineering but a return to the natural forces that used to constrain illegitimacy.

Paragraphs 17-18: Does: Presents first prong of his proposal: penalties against illegitimacy. Says: A single mother with child is not a viable economic unit; therefore cease all government economic aid--except health care--to women with illegitimate children.
Paragraph 19-22: Does: Predicts three good results of withdrawing economic support. Says: (1) more adults will be involved with raising child; (2) more children will be placed for adoption; and (3) social stigma against illegitimacy will be reawakened.

(p. 39). Answers will vary but most students will raise the same kinds of objections contained in the representative list from our own students on p. 41.

(pp. 43-44). These four responses again reveal to students how frequently disagreements among people stem from differences in values, assumptions, and beliefs. Patricia Bucalo objects to Murray because he seems tacitly to accept abortion or at least to consider it a lesser evil than the social problem of neglected or abandoned children. Since "right to life" is one of the typical tenets of political conservatism in the United States, Bucalo feels betrayed that a fellow conservative should be so unconcerned about abortion. In contrast, Pamela Maraldo, who believes in a woman's right to choose abortion, opposes Murray from a liberal standpoint. She objects to Murray's "patronizing and treacherous premise" that girls get pregnant because the think "babies are endearing." To end the cycle of teenage pregnancy, Maraldo proposes better sex education and appropriate economic assistance to eliminate poverty. She also doesn't share Murray's belief that eliminating welfare will lead to adequate care for children provided by families or by orphanages. Instead she sees even more children languishing in poverty and despair. For Maraldo, the problem lies in a racist and poverty-ridden society rather than in an erosion of individual responsibility. Endorsing very different kinds of values, John Leo dismisses the very programs that Maraldo favors: sex education and distribution of condoms, acceptance of diverse kinds of families, and the responsibility of the government to relieve poverty. Assuming that Martin Luther King, Jr. would support Murray's proposal, Leo endorses Murray's plan to restore social stigmas against single-parenthood and return the responsibility of childraising to married couples. For a discussion of Gilliam, see our own analysis of the Murray/Gilliam debate on pp. 48-50 of the text.

Chapter 3

(p. 57). The goal of this exercise is to get students comfortable with freewriting and with sharing their answers. We particularly encourage students to explore the complexity of each of these issues rather than having a set opinion and rationalizing it.

(p. 58). Students enjoy seeing the teacher make a big idea map on the board. The teacher should record every class contribution somewhere on the map. You will need to decide whether an idea should be a new branch off the center circle or a subbranch of a branch already under development. We ask students to help us decide where to put each new idea. It is important, though, not to worry about "correct" placement of ideas on the map. Connecting lines can always be drawn later when students see connections between ideas.

(p. 61). We believe that this is the single most important exercise in this chapter. Peter Elbow's notion of systematic believing and doubting is, to us, an essential feature of argument as clarification. We always like to conduct a discussion of students' metacognitive processes following this exercise. Was it harder to believe this idea or doubt it? Why? Who saw the issue in a different way as a result of having to believe or doubt?

(p. 62). Answers will vary, but the following pro and con because clauses are representative of the kinds of arguments students will raise. At this stage in the course, many of the reasons students put forward will seem illogical, even maddeningly obtuse. We prefer to help students clarify their reasons and articulate the assumptions behind them (preparing for later discussion of warrants), rather than to criticize them. We also praise students who are willing to articulate reasons for a position against which they feel strongly. This is the best way, we say, to learn to see the world through an opposing viewpoint.

1. A student should report a fellow student who is cheating on an exam or plagiarizing an essay.

pro
--because plagiarism or cheating is wrong in principle and shouldn't be condoned by students.
--because condoning plagiarism or cheating reduces the value of good grades earned legitimately.
--because condoning plagiarism or cheating will allow unqualified persons to get positions that would endanger the public (physician who cheated his way through medical school).
--because accepting plagiarism and cheating leads to acceptance of many other sorts of wrong-doing such as shoplifting, cheating on income tax, etc.

con
--because that would be ratting on a fellow student.
--because it is none of my business.
--because the "rules" covering school assignments aren't like real laws that have the consent of the governed.

2. States should legalize marriages between homosexuals.

pro
--because current marriage laws discriminate against sexual minorities.
--because the tax, medical insurance, and other benefits available to heterosexuals entering committed relationships ought to be equally available to homosexuals entering committed relationships.
--because this would be an important step toward ending prejudice against gay people.
--because doing so would make it socially easier for gay people to establish long-term committed relationships and reduce promiscuity.
--because reduction of promiscuity would slow the spread of AIDS.

con
--because doing so would indicate public acceptance of homosexuality.
--because, to the extent that homosexuality is learned rather than inborn, society ought to encourage heterosexuality over homosexuality.
--because homosexuality is opposed to Judeo-Christian values.

--because allowing homosexual marriages would then lead to allowing homosexual couples to adopt children.
--because this is one step toward the complete overthrow of the traditional family.

[See related arguments in the anthology on the topic "Same-Sex Marriage."]

3. Recycling cans, bottles, plastics, and paper does little to help the environment.

pro
--because it is not done to a degree sufficient to make any difference.
--because it distracts us from more pressing national environmental problems
--because it is not economically viable
--because it does not really preserve resources, curb waste or unnecessary consumption

con
--because our natural resources are limited
--because every little bit helps
--because it can be made economically viable
--because it creates jobs
--because none of us wants a landfill in our backyard

[See related arguments in the anthology on the topic "Recycling and Garbage."]

4. Spanking children should be considered child abuse.

pro
--because spanking teaches that it is OK to hit people when you are angry. (Spanking is often an expression of parent anger.)
--because abusive parents often report that they were severely spanked as children.
--because some spanking actually raises welts or causes bruising; because all spanking is harmful psychologically.
--because modern psychology has discovered better ways to discipline children.

con
--because its immediate effect is the best way to teach children not to do dangerous things (cross street, play with matches).

--because it doesn't create long-range guilt.
--because it is easy to tell the difference between spanking as loving, effective discipline (spanking with an open hand that makes an immediate emotional impact without physical harm) and abusive spanking (done with a belt to raise welts).
--because it has long been a tradition in society and considered effective parenting.

5. State and federal governments should legalize hard drugs.
pro
--because doing so would end the black market in drugs and associated criminal activity.
--because the cost of waging the war on drugs is too high.
--because people have a basic right to do what they want to with their own bodies.
--because the more dangerous drugs of alcohol and nicotine are already legal.
--because the revenue from state sale of drugs would add to the general coffers and could be used for providing better treatment for addicts.
con
--because it would lead to public acceptance of hard drugs.
--because it would greatly increase the number of drug addicts.
--because hard drugs would be used at a proportionately higher rate among those without hope in our society and thus would devastate minority communities.
--because the elimination of social constraints against drug use might lead to bad consequences we can't even predict.

[See related arguments in the anthology under the topic "Legalization of Drugs."]

6. For grades 1-12, the school year should be extended to eleven months.
pro
--because doing so would keep our schools competitive with schools in Japan and other countries.
--because the current school year is based on the needs of a now out-of-date agricultural society.
--because the U.S. currently ranks near the bottom of all student achievement categories of first-world countries.

--because it would better utilize school buildings and facilities.
--because the majority of school children now come from single-parent households or households where both parents work, creating enormous childcare problems during the summer.

con
--because psychologically, children need some time off to be kids.
--because the job of being a teacher is now so psychologically demanding and the material rewards so low, that almost no one would go into teaching were it not for the summer vacations.
--because family vacations would be much harder to schedule.
--because the disciplinary problems felt during the regular school year would become intolerable during the hot summer months.

7. Certain advertisements such as the "Joe Camel" cigarette campaign are so immoral they should be made illegal.

pro
--because corporations have an obligation to be socially responsible and when they are not government regulation has to step in.
--because society's responsibility to protect children from unscrupulous advertisers outweighs the "free enterprise" rights of the corporations.
--because precedent already exists in that cigarette ads are banned from TV. It is an easy next step to ban print ads aimed at children.

con
--because it isn't proven that Joe Camel causes children to start smoking.
--because government interference with free enterprise should be minimal.
--because it is impossible to create clear guidelines separating responsible from irresponsible ads. Almost all ads use psychologically strategies to encourage buyers.

8. Violent video games such as Mortal Kombat should be made illegal.

pro
--because they promote violence in children.

--because they make violence fun and thus reduce children's sensitivity to it.
--because they are unwholesome and sick--a sign of a society in decadence.

<u>con</u>
--because kids like them.
--because they sell well and provide high tech jobs.
--because children can distinguish between play and real life and because playing at violence is one way kids come to terms with the violent side of life (traditional kids stories are about being swallowed by wolves or baked in an oven).

9. Rich people are morally obligated to give part of their wealth to the poor.

<u>pro</u>
--because we are all bound by obligations to help those in need.
--because rich people's wealth is partly attributed to "good fortune" and we need to return part to those who have "bad fortune."
--because society in the long run is better off when nobody is poor.
--because altruism is essential to long-term survival of humans.

<u>con</u>
--because giving handouts keeps people from taking responsibility for their own lives.
--because the population explosion will soon eat up the world's capacity to sustain human life and poor countries have much greater population growth than rich countries.
--because people have the right to do what they want with their own money.

[See the dispute between Peter Singer and Garrett Hardin in the anthology on the topic "The Responsibility of the Rich for the Poor."]

10. Women should be assigned to combat duty equally with men.

<u>pro</u>
--because other countries successfully use women in combat roles.
--because women can do the job equally as well as men.
--because not allowing women in combat continues social discrimination against women.

--because not allowing women in combat keeps women from high-level advancement in a military career.

<u>con</u>

--because women should be socialized as nurturers not as killers.
--because, while allowing some exceptions, women cannot perform combat functions as well as men.
--because mixing men and women in combat units would undermine unit cohesiveness and morale.

(p. 63) Exemplified by our discussion of the assertion "Pornography serves a useful function in society" that immediately precedes it, this exercise is particularly useful for instructors who, in an effort to promote the acquisition of an expertise on a particular topic, encourage students to work with the same topic throughout the term, for it suggests ways students can ensure that the topic they choose will not become stale. Consequently, it may be an exercise such instructors will want to direct students to repeatedly throughout the term.

Chapter 4

(pp. 84-85) 1. Information question. 2. Issue-question. See the disagreement between Charles Murray and Dorothy Gilliam on this issue in Chapter 2. 3. Issue-question. Obviously people will disagree about such a values-laden issue as this one. 4. Could be either an issue-question or an information-question. If the audience agrees on a definition of "violence" and on an empirical method for measuring it (as in a social science research study), then this is an information-question. But if the audience disagrees on either the definition of "violence" or on the means of measuring it, then the question will provoke debate. 5. This would be an information-question if a non-controversial answer emerged from social science research. But if several studies disagreed or if an audience found flaws in a study's research design, then the question would become debatable and hence an issue-question. 6. Probably an issue-question even though skeptical medical doctors might prefer to consider it an information-question. 7. This is an information-question calling for an explanation of the different kinds of treatment provided by chiropractors as opposed to medical doctors. 8. An issue-question so long as genuine controversy among experts exists. To the extent, however, that research studies answer this question, the question becomes an information-question. 9. Again, an issue-question so long as medical controversy exists. 10. An issue-question with controversy possible over each of de Beauvoir's operative adjectives: is marriage an outdated institution? an oppressive one? a capitalist one?

(pp. 87-88) 1. Reasonable arguments. Disputants will argue about the criteria for "good" and about whether Lee meets the criteria. 2. Pseudo-arguments. No common assumptions seem possible. 3. Reasonable argument. Writer could establish consequences of subsidizing the convention center and argue that the positive consequences do or do not outweigh the negative ones. 4. Although controversy here is apt to degenerate into pseudo-argument, it is possible to establish rational criteria for "true art" and then to argue that Bozo's painting does or does not meet the criteria. 5. Pseudo-argument. There is probably no way to argue for shared criteria for "attractive." 6. Pseudo-argument--no way to argue for shared criteria for "fun." 7. Possibly a real argument if disputants could point to studies that focus on sharable criteria for "exist." 8. This question differs importantly from question 5 in that "attractive" is now being defined within the context of a specific living room. It is theoretically possible to establish sharable criteria for "attractive" such as "harmony with building architecture," "harmony with furniture elsewhere in house," "harmony with intended contents of room," and so forth. Thus, this question could lead to reasonable argument. 9. Pseudo-argument since no shareable criteria for "better" can be established to compare members of unlike classes of things. 10. Genuine argument since sharable criteria for excellence in an argument essay can be established. (If students doubt this point, consider doing the "norming" exercise in Appendix Two.)

(p. 91) We consider this an important collaborative exercise because it gives students practice composing "because clauses" for their own claims and because it encourages students to see the power of opposing positions.

Chapter 5

(p. 98) 1. <u>Claim</u>: We shouldn't elect Joe as committee chair. <u>Stated Reason</u>: because he is too bossy. <u>Unstated assumption</u>: People who are too bossy make poor committee chairs. 2. <u>Claim</u>: You should buy this stereo system. <u>Stated reason</u>: because it has a powerful amplifier. <u>Unstated assumption</u>: If a stereo system has a powerful amplifier, you should buy it. 3. <u>Claim</u>: Drugs should not be legalized. <u>Stated reason</u>: because legalization would greatly increase the number of drug addicts. <u>Unstated assumption</u>: We should not pass legislation that increases the number of drug addicts. (Increasing the number of drug addicts is bad.) 4. <u>Claim</u>: Practicing the piano is good for kids. <u>Stated reason</u>: because it teaches discipline. <u>Unstated assumption</u>: Activities that teach discipline are good for kids. 5. <u>Claim</u>: Welfare benefits for unwed mothers should be eliminated. <u>Stated reason</u>: because doing so will greatly reduce the nation's illegitimacy rate. <u>Unstated assumption</u>: Legislation that reduces the illegitimacy rate should be passed. (It is good to reduce the nation's illegitimacy rate.) 6. <u>Claim</u>: Welfare benefits for unwed mothers should not be eliminated. <u>Stated reason</u>: because welfare benefits are needed to prevent unbearable poverty among our nation's most helpless citizens. <u>Unstated assumption</u>: Assistance that prevents unbearable poverty should not be eliminated. (Preventing poverty is good.) 7. <u>Claim</u>: We should strengthen the Endangered Species Act. <u>Stated reason</u>: because doing so will preserve genetic diversity on the planet. <u>Unstated assumption</u>: We should preserve genetic diversity on the planet. 8. <u>Claim</u>: The Endangered Species Act is too stringent. <u>Stated reason</u>: because it severely damages the economy. <u>Unstated assumption</u>: Laws and regulations that severely damage the economy are too stringent. (It is bad to severely damage the economy.) 9. <u>Claim</u>: The doctor should not perform an abortion in this case. <u>Stated reason</u>: because the mother's life is not in danger. <u>Unstated Assumption</u>: Abortions should only be performed in those cases when the mother's life is in danger. 10. Answers will vary: <u>Claim</u>: Abortion should be legal. <u>Stated reason</u>: because a woman has the right to control her own body. <u>Unstated assumptions</u>: All persons have a right to control their own bodies. Since abortion is an act of control over one's own body, abortions are a right. Thus abortions should be legal.

(p. 106) 1. Done in text. 2. <u>Claim</u>: You should buy this stereo system. <u>Stated reason</u>: because it has a powerful amplifier. <u>Grounds</u>: All available specs showing that this is a powerful amplifier. <u>Warrant</u>: A powerful amplifier is the main criterion you should use to determine which amplifier to buy. <u>Backing</u>: Since a powerful amplifier will drive the biggest speakers; since powerful amplifiers have strong prestige value; since powerful amplifiers have less distortion at low volume levels. <u>Qualifier</u>: Other things being equal. <u>Conditions of Rebuttal</u>: Unless the power of the amplifier isn't the main criterion (perhaps cost, ease of operation, reliability, appearance, other specs are more important than power).

3. <u>Claim</u>: Drugs should not be legalized. <u>Stated reason</u>: because legalization would greatly increase the number of drug addicts. <u>Grounds</u>: Evidence that more people would use drugs if they were cheap and legal; comparative data showing rise in alcoholism after repeal of prohibition. <u>Warrant</u>: We should not pass legislation that increases the number of drug addicts. <u>Backing</u>: Evidence and arguments showing the harm caused by addiction. <u>Qualifier</u>: probably. <u>Conditions of rebuttal</u>: Unless aggressive education programs made use of drugs socially unacceptable; unless the benefits of eliminating the black market outweighed the negative effects of more addicts.

4. <u>Claim</u>: Practicing the piano is good for kids. <u>Stated reason</u>: because it teaches discipline. <u>Grounds</u>: Evidence that practicing the piano develops discipline. <u>Warrant</u>: Learning discipline is important for kids. <u>Backing</u>: Since practicing discipline develops good work habits, teaches lesson that short-term fun must sometimes be sacrificed for long-term gains, develops habits that can be transferred to other areas of life, and so forth. <u>Qualifier</u>: For most kids. <u>Conditions of Rebuttal</u>: Unless practicing piano doesn't really teach discipline; unless costs outweigh this benefit; unless habit of mind doesn't really transfer to other areas.

5. <u>Claim</u>: Welfare benefits for unwed mothers should be eliminated. <u>Stated reason</u>: because doing so will greatly reduce the nation's illegitimacy rate. <u>Grounds</u>: Arguments that social stigmas will again be placed on unwed mothers, leading to reduction in out-of-wedlock births. <u>Warrant</u>: Legislation that reduces the illegitimacy rate should be passed. (It is good to reduce the nation's illegitimacy rate.) <u>Backing</u>: Arguments that

two-parent families provide a securer home for children; evidence that illegitimacy rate correlates with rise in crime, drug use, school dropouts. Qualifier: quite likely. Conditions of Rebuttal: Unless receipt of welfare benefits isn't an incentive to have children; unless poverty and crime cause illegitimacy instead of vice versa; unless the harm done to children is too great.

6. Claim: Welfare benefits for unwed mothers should not be eliminated. Stated reason: because welfare benefits are needed to prevent unbearable poverty among our nation's most helpless citizens. Grounds: Evidence of the kinds of misery that would be caused by elimination of welfare benefits. Warrant: Assistance that prevents unbearable poverty should not be eliminated. Backing: Arguments showing that we have a moral obligation to relieve poverty. Qualifier: quite likely. Conditions of Rebuttal: Unless elimination of welfare wouldn't create more poverty (families and charities might take up the slack, illegitimacy rate might rapidly decline); unless we don't have an obligation to relieve poverty (perhaps the resulting increase in poverty would be only temporary and then free enterprise would relieve it).

7. Claim: We should strengthen the Endangered Species Act. Stated reason: because doing so will preserve genetic diversity on the planet. Grounds: Evidence that without the Act genetic diversity is being lost, that the act is sustaining it, and that a strengthened act would be more effective. Warrant: We should preserve genetic diversity on the planet. Backing: Arguments showing why genetic diversity is an important value. Qualifier: with few exceptions. Conditions of Rebuttal: Unless even a strengthened Endangered Species Act wouldn't preserve much genetic diversity; unless genetic diversity on the planet isn't really threatened; unless genetic diversity isn't really important or as important as other factors such as the economy.

8. Claim: The Endangered Species Act is too stringent. Stated reason: because it severely damages the economy. Grounds: Evidence and arguments showing that the Act severely damages the economy. Warrant: Laws and regulations that severely damage the economy are too stringent. Backing: Arguments showing why it is bad to damage the economy; arguments showing that preservation of the economy is more important than preserving genetic diversity.

Qualifier: with few exceptions. Conditions of Rebuttal: Unless the Endangered Species Act doesn't really damage the economy; unless the harm to the economy can be readily reversed; unless the long-range dangers of reduced genetic diversity outweigh the damage to the economy.

9. Claim: The doctor should not perform an abortion in this case. Stated reason: because the mother's life is not in danger. Grounds: Evidence, including the testimony of other doctors, showing that the mother's life is not in danger. Warrant: Abortions should only be performed in those cases when the mother's life is in danger. Backing: Argument showing why this criterion is necessary. Qualifier: In most cases. Conditions of Rebuttal: Unless the mother's life is in danger; unless there are other occasions when abortions should be performed.

10. Claim: Abortion should be legal. Stated reason: because a woman has the right to control her own body. Grounds: Argument that abortion is an act of control over one's own body. Warrant: One has a legal right to control one's body. Backing: Argument showing why control over one's body should be a right. Qualifier: Even though a right, abortion shouldn't be as ethically free as having a tooth pulled. Conditions of Rebuttal: Unless a fetus isn't part of the woman's body; unless control over one's body isn't a right.

(p. 112) 1.a. To show the annoyance of sales taxes, the writer could provide personal experiences about carrying around pocketfuls of change, of having dresser drawers full of pennies, of never being able quickly to figure out the price of something, of forgetting to include sales tax in consideration of big ticket expenses, and so forth. 1.b. As examples of Professor X's ineffective homework assignments, the writer could cite Professor X's busywork fill-in-the-blank problems, his rewarding of pointless extra credit homework such as tracing and coloring maps, and his preference for boilerplated book reports. 1.c. For example, last Tuesday afternoon Professor X spent two hours with Theresa and then went over to her house in the evening to talk personally with her parents. The week before Professor X had helped Sam look for a job and excused Sally from an exam because of Sally's concern for her grandmother's illness.

2.a. Annoying taxes cause resentment against government, and they encourage cheating. 2.b. Through effective homework teachers create independent, self-motivated learners. This is a far more important educational outcome than, say, making students laugh. 2.c. Teachers need to be role models for their students, and it is rare indeed for a student to see caring altruistic behavior from a teacher. Such a teacher instructs students in lifelong values--a benefit that may exceed mere book learning.

Chapter 6

(p. 127) The purpose of this exercise is to afford students an opportunity to practice making the kinds of decisions that one must be make when attempting to translate data into graphs and to experience the difficulties of doing so first-hand. Informing their decisions about how to construct the various graphs should be a careful study of the section, "Using Graphs for Effect," on pp. 124-126 of this chapter. Sharing and comparing the graphs they create with the class as a whole is sure to provide opportunities for fruitful discussion.

(p. 128) This exercise is designed to alert students to the various ways the same set of numbers can be employed and manipulated to support entirely different claims. Those opposed to the proposed ballpark would probably cite the last three statements in support of their claim, for these seem to emphasize the considerable cost of the construction, while those in favor would probably cite the first three insofar as they essentially minimize that cost.

(p. 137) "There seemed to be considerable satisfaction with the library as a quiet place to study. In response to our questionnaire, 50 percent of respondents agreed or strongly agreed that the library was a quiet place to study while only 10 percent strongly disagreed."
"Students seem dissatisfied with the noise level of the library. In response to our questionnaire only 10 percent of students felt strongly that the library was a quiet place to study while fully 45 percent felt the library was not a quiet place to study."

Chapter 7

(pp. 148-149) 1.a. Warrant: Whatever all my friends are allowed to do I should be allowed to do. 1.b. Warrant: Parental concessions that encourage my maturity are desireable. [Example 1.b is more audience-based; it appeals to a value that parents typically hope to inspire in their children rather than a value typically prized by a child.] 2.a. Warrant: People who want to spend the summer in the mountains and who like to ride horses would be good candidates for a summer job at the Happy Trails Dude Ranch. 2.b. Warrant: People who have had considerable experience serving others in volunteer work and who know how to make guests feel welcome and relaxed would be good candidates for a summer job at the Happy Trails Dude Ranch. [Example 2.b is more audience-based; it appeals to the values that the employer is looking for in an employee rather than the values that the employee is looking for.] 3.a. Warrant: An evaluation system should prepare people for the competitive world of business. 3.b. Warrant: An evaluation system should tell students that there are certain standards of excellence that must be met if individuals are to reach their full potential. [Example 3.b. is more audience-based since the argument is aimed at persons opposed to competition. The mention of the words "full potential" in the second argument is apt to appeal to the target audience since opponents of competition are frequently supporters of self-growth and fulfillment.] 4.a. Warrant: Maintaining a healthy heart is very important. 4.b. Warrant: Eliminating the suffering of animals is very important. [4.b. probably most appeals to the values of young people from 15 to 25; they are apt to be more moved by appeals to animal suffering than to healthy hearts.] 5.a. Warrant: Anything that promotes public acceptance of homosexuality is good. 5.b. Warrant: Anything that makes it easier for gay people to establish and sustain long-term stable relationships is good. [Probably example 5.b. is more audience-based insofar as long-term stable relationships represent a "family value."]

(p. 147) Answers will vary, but the following approaches are suggestive. 1. <u>Problem</u>: Parents are afraid that violent video games will harm their children by teaching them violence. <u>Possible Solutions</u>: Show that good kids play these games without psychological harm and that many classic children's stories are violent. Try to reduce parents' fear that the games are harmful. Argue that the games are fun and challenging and that success at them builds self-confidence. Try to emphasize other good effects from parents' perspective. [This is a good opportunity to raise questions about sophistry versus real clarification of a complex issue. In our experience, many students love these violent video games and argue passionately that they don't do harm. In contrast, the authors of this book hate violent video games and feel "tainted" in trying to argue their case.] 2. Problem: It is fairly easy to make a case to the general public for limiting the number of terms that can be served by members of congress. One standard approach is a "throw the bums out" strategy that emphasizes the fat cat networks established by long-term congresspeople. But the audience specified in this task are people who support an influential incumbent and thus risk losing the benefits of that person's power in congress. Possible solutions: One approach is to appeal to long-term rather than short-term benefits based on the good of the whole country rather than that of partisan supporters. More narrowly, one might argue that dependence on political influence in congress is always fragile and that the elimination of a partisan system might encourage regions and companies to develop a broader economic base. [For all these issues, it is impossible to come up with specific arguments without extensive research of particular cases. Stress this point with students. The purpose of the current exercise is to help students see strategies for approaching an argument. The goal is find arguments that appeal to the audience's values.] 3. Problem: Raising gasoline tax to promote energy conservation works only if it reduces the amount of driving that people do. But much highway driving is necessary, not voluntary--particularly trucking to deliver consumer goods. Business leaders are worried that the gasoline tax, which will be passed on to consumers in the form of higher prices, will hurt the economy. Possible solutions: Once again, appealing to long-range rather than short-range benefits might be useful. Sooner or later another oil crisis is inevitable. Raising gas taxes now constitutes a gradualist approach that may stave off a disastrous crisis later. The key strategy here is to find business-oriented rather than environmentalist reasons for supporting the gasoline tax. Students may come up with additional hypotheses for how a gasoline tax might be good for business in the long run. 4. <u>Problem</u>: Subscribers to <u>Reader's Digest</u> are generally older, conservative people who have an antipathy against drugs and the lifestyles they symbolize. They generally support the war on drugs, desire mobilization of police against drug users, and want to lock up bigtime dealers for life. The legalization of cocaine, to them, might symbolize the complete disintegration of society. <u>Possible solutions</u>: A good strategy here is to emphasize the social benefits of legalization: freeing police to focus on violent crime; eliminating the black market that drives a large percentage of street crime; taking the glamour and profit out of drug dealing, thus encouraging the underclass toward middle class values.

(p. 157) Answers will vary, but the following suggestions can be used to help guide class discussion. 1.a. Here the writer's purpose is to create sympathy for the use of animals in biomedical research. Thus the opening scene might focus on the happy benefit of a cured child rather than the suffering of an animal. Perhaps the writer could show a smiling child recovering from extensive burn wounds healed through research using animals. For an even more pathetic appeal, the scene might include "before" and "after" elements so that the reader is made to "see and feel" the burns themselves. 1.b. Now the opening scene should create sympathy for the "animal rights" side of the controversy. An effective ploy might be to describe the suffering of a rabbit during an eye sensitivity test for cosmetics or a monkey's screaming in pain during some medical research procedure. 2.a. The essay could open with a description of a formerly beautiful vista now marred by thousands of campers and R.V.s. 2.b. A similar scene except now the writer would focus not on lost beauty but on the plight, say, of a harried couple having to pitch their tent between two R.V.s equipped with stereo systems. 3.a. The scene could describe a high-rolling drug dealer driving a Porsche and wearing glittering rings and bracelets. The point would be that legalization would put this dude out of business. 3.b. Here the writer could describe a heroin addict in a back alley injecting drugs, his life hopeless and full of despair. The argument would continue by suggesting that legalization would lead to more people in the same plight.

(p. 163) This class discussion activity works most effectively if students have not yet read the whole of Chapter 7. We usually have students do this exercise on the same day that we assign Chapter 7. In class we ask them to read both versions of Goodman's essay and then to do this exercise. 1.a. If something degrades and humiliates women, then it discriminates against women and thus should be illegal. Pornography degrades and humiliates women. Therefore pornography discriminates against women and thus should be illegal. 1.b. The Minneapolis Ordinance is a bad law because it has potentially dangerous consequences. 2. Most students say that version 2 is most useful in answering these questions. 3. Most students prefer version 1. Class discussion about "why" is usually quite fruitful. Further discussion occurs within the text.

Chapter 8

(p. 169) Answers will vary. What you want to get students to see at the beginning is that one version summarizes an opposing view while the other version doesn't. It is useful to get students to share their reactions to one-sided versus two-sided arguments.

(p. 174) Answers will vary. It is useful here to have the students read their summaries aloud (or prepare them in working groups on transparencies for sharing on an overhead projector), and then identify the features that make each version either loaded or fair.

(p. 177) 1. <u>Warrant</u>: Grading systems that encourage creativity should be selected. <u>Grounds</u>: Evidence that students would be more creative under a pass-fail system. <u>Backing</u>: Arguments for why creativity is such an important criterion. <u>Conditions of Rebuttal</u>: Attack grounds by showing that students would be less apt to be creative under a pass-fail system; attack the warrant by showing that criteria other than creativity are more important. 2. <u>Warrant</u>: Any substance that causes cancer and heart disease should be made illegal by the government. <u>Grounds</u>: Evidence that cigarettes cause cancer and heart disease. <u>Backing</u>: Arguments that the government should make any substance that causes cancer and heart disease illegal. <u>Conditions of Rebuttal</u>: Attack the grounds by showing, if possible, that cigarettes have not be proven by themselves to cause cancer and heart disease; attack the warrant by showing how freedom of the individual outweighs the state's duty to withhold potentially dangerous substances from its people (will the state next outlaw doughnuts as detrimental to our health?)   3.   <u>Warrant</u>: Financial payoff is the primary criterion for determining the value of a major.   <u>Grounds</u>: Evidence that engineers make more money than music majors. <u>Backing</u>: Arguments showing that income levels are the chief measure of the value of a major. <u>Conditions of Rebuttal</u>: Attack the grounds by showing that many music majors earn more money than engineers.   Attack the warrant by arguing for criteria other than financial payoff.   4.   <u>Warrant</u>: Any activity that causes needless pain and suffering to animals ought to be avoided.   <u>Grounds</u>: Evidence that our eating of meat causes animals needless pain and suffering. <u>Backing</u>: Arguments that activities that cause animals needless pain and suffering should be avoided.   <u>Conditions of Rebuttal</u>: Attack grounds by showing that the eating of meat either does not or need not cause animals needless pain and suffering; attack warrant by showing that some activities causing pain and suffering to animals are necessary.   5. <u>Warrant</u>:   Laws that seriously hamper the economy are too stringent. <u>Grounds</u>: Evidence that the endangered species law seriously hampers the economy. <u>Backing</u>: Arguments that a vigorous economy is more important to the long-range survival of humans than the existence of endangered species. <u>Conditions of Rebuttal</u>: Attack grounds by arguing that the endangered species law isn't really hampering the economy; attack warrant by arguing that the existence of endangered species is a greater good than the short-range economic benefits that might occur if we lessened the law's rigor.

(p. 181) 1. Issue addressed: Is abstract art really art? 2. Writer's claim: Abstract art is really art, requiring just as much artistic talent and creativity as representational art. 3. Opposing view: Abstract art is not really art because it does not represent the artist's technical drafting skills, because it does not represent orderly, logical composition, and because it does not portray the ideal and the real. 4. Writer's refutation: many abstract artists are excellent draftsmen; a work of art need not be logical and aesthetically pleasing to be art; and abstract artists do portray the real, that is, reality as the artist interprets it.

(p. 186) 1. Shared values: Both sides have the best interests of the store and its customers at heart; both recognize that the cost of the initial investment is not a factor in the decision; both value classical music and "the culture that [the] store brings to Grayfish"; both share certain fears about introducing an inventory of electronic music equipment to the store. 2. As a classical argument, the letter would have a "self-announcing structure" such that its introduction would present the issue, provide any necessary background, and announce the writer's thesis; in the body of the letter, the writer would present her own reasons and evidence in support of her position and summarize and refute the opposing views of her employer. It would be useful, of course, to prompt students to consider which form of argument would be the better one for enabling the writer to accomplish her purpose with her designated audience, and why.

Chapter 9

(pp. 196-197) Answers will vary, but the following illustrative responses will be useful for generating discussion.

1.a. Marijuana should be legalized because marijuana is a natural, organic substance, because possessing marijuana is a victimless "crime," because people who want to smoke marijuana are primarily law-abiding, responsible citizens (principle/definition); because legalizing marijuana will have these good consequences: increased tax revenues, decriminalization of many people's recreational activities, and the growth of a new profitable agricultural industry (cause/consequence); because prohibiting marijuana is as futile as was prohibiting alcohol, because drinking alcohol is legal and yet is demonstrably more harmful than smoking marijuana (resemblance).

1.b. Division I college athletes should receive salaries because they perform the same function for their schools as professional athletes do for their organizations; because they deserve just compensation for their talent, skills, and the degree of commitment that college athletics requires them to have to their sport (principle/definition); because receiving a salary might enable them to provide their families with the financial support that their absence from home otherwise deprives their families of; because receiving a salary while a college athlete might encourage more college athletes to stay in school through to graduation (cause/consequence); because paying college athletes for services rendered is like paying any one else for a particular skill or expertise, or like paying any other entertainer (resemblance).

1.c. Couples should live together before getting married because living together is a test of commitment in today's climate of divorce (principle/definition); because living together will lead to these good consequences: a more mature and responsible sense of marriage, fewer divorces, and greater sexual health among young people (cause/consequence); because breaking up after living together is like getting divorced after a brief marriage but with fewer bad consequences, because living together before marriage is like a shakedown hike before starting into the wilderness area (resemblance).

1.d. The United States should end its energy dependence on other nations because we are a proud nation that should be self-sufficient, because the communal good of eliminating our deficit trade balance outweighs the individual good of cheaper gasoline (principle); because energy independence will lead to these good consequences: reduced federal trade deficit, greater national security, improvement of the environment from reduced energy consumption, stimulation of creativity in finding alternatives to petroleum energy, greater national pride, less need to be the world's policemen (cause/consequence); because ending our dependence on others for oil is like a family's owning their own home rather than having to rent, because the United States' dependence on others for oil is like California's dependence on other's for water--you live in continual fear of events beyond your control (resemblance).

e.-i. Reverse the arguments. Here is one example:

Marijuana should not be legalized because marijuana is more dangerous than many people realize, because the desire of some people to smoke marijuana doesn't outweigh society's general interest in preventing public acceptance of another dangerous drug (principle/definition); because legalizing marijuana would have these bad consequences: increased use of marijuana throughout the country, greater temptation to use even more dangerous drugs, glamorization of a drug-dependent way of life, increased health risks from the known dangers of marijuana (cause/consequence); because legalizing marijuana will set a precedent for legalizing cocaine and heroin (resemblance).

2. Answers will vary. Teachers can count this exercise successful if they sense that students are producing more lines of reasoning than they might otherwise produce. Students shouldn't worry whether a particular reason exactly fits one of the three slots. Stress that the purpose of this exercise is suggestive only; it prods writers to explore several different avenues into an argument.

Chapter 10

(p. 202) 1. What is a creative act? (criteria issue). Does childbirth meet these criteria? (match issue). 2. What is vandalism? Does writing graffiti on subways meet these criteria? 3. What is a true language? Does porpoise "language" meet these criteria? 4. What are the criteria for a "sexist event"? Does a beauty contest meet these criteria? 5. What is a precise definition of a "carnival amusement ride"? (criteria issue). Does bungee jumping from a crane meet these criteria? (match issue). 6. What is a true science? Does psychology meet these criteria? 7. What is a creative activity? Does designing T.V. advertisements meet these criteria? 8. What are the criteria for determining the "true mother" of a child? Does a surrogate mother meet these criteria? 9. What is an athlete? Do cheerleaders meet these criteria? 10. What is a game of luck? Does poker meet these criteria?

(pp. 207-208) Answers will vary on some of the problems. 1. presence of gills is a necessary criterion (all fish have gills) but not a sufficient criterion for fish (tadpoles have gills also). 2. Having yellow hair is a necessary and sufficient criterion for being a blond. 3. Being born within the U.S. is a sufficient criterion for American citizenship (you are automatically an American citizen if you are born within the boundaries of the U.S.) but not a necessary one (you can become a naturalized citizen). 4. Being over 65 is a sufficient criterion but not a necessary one (all states say that "senior citizenship" is in effect at 65 but some say at 62 or even at 55). 5. Everyone will agree that knowing several programming languages is not a necessary criterion for meeting the foreign language requirement; however, a university might have heated debates about whether it is a sufficient criterion. 6. Having rhyming line endings is neither a necessary criterion for a poem (many poems don't rhyme) nor a sufficient one (many language constructs that rhyme aren't true poems). 7. Teaching classes at a college is neither a necessary nor sufficient criterion for being a college professor. 8. Eating no meat, ever, is a sufficient criterion for being a vegetarian, but many people would argue it is not a necessary one (since some vegetarians eat some meat). 9. Killing another human being is a necessary criterion for murder but not a sufficient one. 10. Most people would agree that a good sex life is not a sufficient criterion for a happy marriage (other factors are important too); it is probably arguable whether a good sex life is a necessary criterion.

(p. 211) This is an important exploration activity for students writing a definitional essay in response to our assignment on p. 200. A full discussion of this activity is found in the following NCTE research booklet: Johannessen, Larry R., Elizabeth A. Kahn, and Carolyn Calhoun Walter, <u>Designing and Sequencing Prewriting Activities</u>, Urbana, IL: NCTE, 1982. This activity is adapted from the booklet. 1. and 2. Student answers, of course, will vary. Most groups, however, arrive at similar conclusions. Here is a typical conclusion. For an act to be courageous it must meet the following criteria: (1) it must involve risk of something of value (usually one's life, but occasionally one's reputation as in the case of Mutt and Jeff); (2) it must be done consciously with the doer being aware of the danger; (3) it must be done reasonably with some hope of success (ruling out the case of the foolhardy parent in case d.); (4) it must be done for a noble purpose (ruling out the teenager saving the memento in case c., the mountain climbers in case e., and the bank robbers in case f.). Most groups believe that the fireman in case b. is courageous but not as courageous as the neighbor in case a. since the neighbor faces greater risk of harm. This is a difference of degree rather than kind. 3. Answers will vary.

(p. 214) Answers will vary. Here are some typical responses:
1. a. <u>Obvious examples of cruelty to animals</u>: torturing an animal for the fun of it; going out of your way to hit an animal while driving your car; starving your pet gerbils through neglect. b. <u>Contrastive examples</u>: causing suffering to animals for a significant human reason (medical research); accidentally hitting an animal while driving your car; discovering a gerbil starved to death in your drawer when you didn't know where the gerbil was. c. <u>Borderline cases</u>: Causing animals to suffer for scientific research of questionable value (development of lipsticks or hair shampoo); squirrel hunting; catch-and-release fishing; stepping on ants; branding cattle; drowning newborn kittens.
2. Through conversation, students will generally discover that at least four criteria are involved in a definition of cruelty to animals: (1) <u>intention</u>--intentionally harming an animal versus accidentally harming an animal; (2) <u>adequate human need or purpose</u>--killing for food, medical research, protection of property versus killing or maiming for the fun of it or for inadequate purpose; (3) <u>limiting suffering to absolute minimum</u>--killing a deer quickly and cleanly versus letting it suffer, using anesthetics in medical research versus absence of anesthetics; and (4) <u>relative "worth" of the animal</u>--killing a gopher in your yard versus killing a squirrel in your yard, killing starlings versus killing robins, killing squawfish versus killing trout (this last criterion always raises troubling issues of human-centrism).

Typical theses statements might be as follows:

"Although the father in the Starling Case intentionally killed the birds, his act is not cruelty to animals because the psychological harm to the family justified their getting rid of the starlings, because starlings are damage-causing pests, and because no other means of solving the problem, short of killing the birds in this way, was possible."   [or]

"The Starling Case involves cruelty to the animals because the father intentionally killed the birds without adequate justification, because he caused needless suffering in doing so, and because, despite the claim of some classmates, starlings are as deserving of life as robins or kittens."

(p. 219) 1. See our analyses of the Sullivan and Krauthammer essays in the "Analysis of Readings" section of this Instructor's Manual. 2a. confinable according to both present and proposed criteria: a severely depressed streetperson with a hunting knife threatening to kill himself and unable to talk coherently. 2b. confinable according to Krauthammer's degradation criterion but not the current danger criterion: the same person as above but without the hunting knife and the suicide threats; a person with bizarre, incoherent behavior, especially if accompanied with bad hygiene, could be involuntarily hospitalized under Krauthammer's criterion, even if the person posed no threat to himself or others. 2c. not confinable by either criteria: a person whose mental illness was not readily apparent and didn't lead to behaviors that middle-class citizens would find "degrading." 3. Putting limits on who could be confined involuntarily is one of the obvious problems raised by Krauthammer's proposal. Perhaps more specific criteria could be established and a board of psychologists could review each case. For example, bizarre behavior might be involuntarily confinable only if the person became physically degraded as a result of mental illness (soiled with feces and urine) or if the person became an intolerable nuisance (not simply conducting an invisible symphony on a street corner but going continually into stores and restaurants shouting obscenities).

Chapter 11

(p. 240) Answers will vary. Here are some possibilities: 1.a. Invention of the automobile enables commuting, which leads to creation of suburbs, which in turn leads to freeways and shopping centers. 1.b. Invention of the automobile creates opportunities for teenagers to get away from adult chaperons by driving to a remote place; automobile becomes a transportable "bedroom." 1.c Elvis Presley's arrival brings rock and roll to the nation creating for the first time a "generation gap" in musical taste. The rhythms and lyrics of rock and roll music create an atmosphere of rebellion against uptight middle class values. The new teenage subculture is ripe for experimentation with drugs in the 1960s. The values of the "flower children" are carried in the music. 1.d. The invention of the telephone makes it possible to keep in touch with people over a distance. For the first time you could talk with your friends when they were not present. Consequently, people had less emotional need to know their neighbors since friendship networks were now different from neighborhood networks. Talking to your friends via telephone reduced your need to develop a sense of community in your neighborhood. 1.e. The development of the "pill" in the 1960s led to a new sense of freedom from worry about pregnancy. This sense of freedom, in turn, contributed to the rise in premarital and extramarital sex. This sexual revolution was accompanied by an increase in the divorce rate as more and more spouses became dissatisfied with their marital partners. 1.f. The development of a way to prevent rejections in transplant operations led to a rapid increase in the number of transplants being performed, which led, in turn, to a greater need for donors of organs. Because of the scarcity of transplantable organs left intact from fatal accidents, social pressure mounted to use organs from people who desired death by euthanasia. This social pressure led to enactment of more liberal euthanasia laws.

2.a. example answer in text. 2.b. The invention of the automobile led to changes in sexual mores because the automobile became a transportable bedroom that allowed couples privacy away from chaperons. 2.c. Elvis Presley's arrival and introduction of rock and roll to the nation contributed to the rise of the drug culture in the 1960s because it created a teenage subculture founded on rebellion against middle class values, making teenagers ripe for experimentation with drugs. 2.d. The invention of the telephone damaged a sense of community in neighborhoods because the telephone enabled people to maintain networks of friends at a distance, thus lessening people's dependence on neighborhoods. 2.e. The development of the pill fueled the rising divorce rate because it provided freedom from pregnancy, which led to the sexual revolution and dissatisfaction with the restrictions of marriage. 2.f. The development of a way to prevent rejections in transplant operations led to liberalization of euthanasia laws because the increased demand for transplant operations increased the demand for organ donors.

(p. 244) 1. Perhaps daily meditation causes a reduction in stress; but perhaps the kind of person who enjoys daily meditation is already someone with low stress levels so that there is no causal connection at all between the correlated phenomena. 2. A person who regularly consumes frozen dinners may be a person with very little free time to fix meals. Such a person may be a harried commuter who will vote for rapid transit in order to increase time to be at home. 3. Social scientists disagree about why first born children tend to be high achievers. The most common explanations include more parental attention in early years, more family responsibility placed on them, more rewards from parents to serve as role models for siblings, and so forth. 4. Unlike most "hobby organizations" such as gardening clubs, the National Rifle Association has become a major political force lobbying against gun control legislation. Its members see gun control as government intrusion on individual rights, a conservative stance that they extend to treatment of criminals and other issues.

(pp. 245-246) 1. answers will vary. 2. answers will also vary. Here are some possibilities: b. Why teenagers don't listen to classical music: It is hard to think of immediate and precipitating causes for the absence of a phenomenon; contributing causes (extreme peer pressure to listen to rock, lack of education about classical music, association of classical music with effete people, association of classical music with values very unlike teenage values); remote causes (rise of rock subculture, long tradition of popular as opposed to classical music in the United States, rise of phonographs which made "non-live" music available and the subsequent drop in the number of people who played musical instruments themselves; popularity of bands rather than orchestras in high schools); constraints (peer pressure, lack of role models). c. Why the number of babies born out of wedlock has increased dramatically in the last thirty years: precipitating cause for a particular case (teenage girl has fight with mother); immediate cause (girl goes to boyfriend for comfort, sympathy turns to passion, goes too far, has no birth control); contributing causes (lack of happiness at home, increased number of friends who are active sexually, peer pressure to lose virginity, belief that "I won't get pregnant this time," perhaps unacknowledged desire to get pregnant as a way of getting back at parents or forcing boyfriend into marriage); remote causes (breakdown of older sexual values, troubles at home, loss of religious influences on behavior, movies and advertisements glamorizing sex); constraints (fear of pregnancy, parental disapproval, desire to make sex meaningful, lack of birth control, lack of appropriate place). For a deepening of this discussion, return to the debate surrounding Charles Murray's proposal to eliminate welfare benefits for single parents (Chapter 2) and the section on "Illegitimacy, Single Parenthood, and Welfare Reform" in the anthology. Murray claims that a strong contributing cause to illegitimacy is the welfare benefit that brings money to unwed mothers and reduces social constraints against teenage pregnancy. Countering Murray are arguments that poverty and hopelessness lead to family instability.

(p. 252) For a discussion of Minot's essay, as well as the essays by Sagan, Torpey, and Fuchs, see the "Analysis of Readings" section of this Instructor's Manual.

Chapter 12

(pp. 270-271) Answers will vary. Here are some possibilities: a. Spanking a child to teach obedience is like blackmailing a mate into fidelity: it makes people act out of fear rather than love. b. Building low cost housing for poor people is like Jesus's clothing the naked: compassionate and just [or] Building low cost housing for poor people is like burning paper for warmth: it works for a while but soon the problem returns. c. The use of steroids by college athletes is like putting herbicide on a dandelion: it makes it grow vigorously for a short time and then kills it. d. Mandatory AIDS testing for all U.S. residents is like strip searching all residents for smuggled drugs every six months: demeaning, unconstitutional, and unlikely to solve the problem. e. For the federal government to eliminate all federally subsidized student loans is like a logging and paper company eliminating the replanting of clearcut forests: it saves money short term but eventually destroys the very basis of revenue. f. The effects of fast food on our health is like the effects of putting sugar in your car's gas tank: your car will run for a while but eventually the engine will get clogged and seize up. g. Profiting from a book about your illegal activities is like inheriting money from a relative you murdered: it promotes evil and rewards unproductive behavior.

(pp. 273-274) 1.a. Are there examples of governors who have been effective presidents? Is Governor Frick different from other governors so that he is an exception to the rule? Were previous governors who became presidents inferior in other ways so that no general rule about governors can be formulated? 1.b To what extent should the United States follow precedents set by other Western countries? Are there differences in the social structure of the U.S. and other Western countries that should make U.S. military policy on gays different from policies of other countries? Are there differences in demands made on the military in the U.S.? Have there been any problems with gays in the military in other Western countries? 1.C. In what way is the former Yugoslavia different from Vietnam? In what way are the American people in the 1990s different from the American people in the late 1960s so that the war might have a different impact on the people? Did we learn anything from Vietnam that would allow us to intervene in Eastern Europe differently? 2. What actually happened in Massachusetts and California? What kind of initiative did they pass in those states. What effect did those initiatives have on the economies of those states? Specifically, what effect did those initiatives have on public services? How is the economy of Montana different from the economies of those states? How is Montana's initiative similar or different from those passed in other states?

(pp. 276-277) 1. Kilpatrick draws an analogy between providing a urine specimen for an employer and being checked for weapons at an airplane terminal. To the extent that the reader agrees with the necessity of searching for weapons at an airport, the analogy is quite compelling. But what are the differences between a drug search by urinalysis and a weapons search by metal detector? In the latter case, authorities are looking for terrorists who provide a clear, unambiguous danger to all other airline passengers. Guiltless people can see that the search clearly protects them, and it offers little in the way of disruption to their daily lives. In the drug case, however, the danger is less clear and compelling. Moreover, "guilty" persons are not terrorists, but persons who choose to use recreational drugs. In part, at least, the search is aimed at attacking a life style. Much more so than in the airline case, mandatory urinalysis tests are searches without a search warrant. There is reason to waive the protection of unreasonable searches in the case of the airlines because of the overwhelming danger, but there is no such danger sufficient to waive it in the case of employee drug testing.

2. People who support affirmative action tend to find Greenberg's analogies compelling: there is a clear resemblance between distinguishing between two qualified persons on the basis of race and making similar distinctions on the basis of seniority, geographic diversity, or veteran status. In each case, the general social good or the general good of the institution becomes a selection criterion when distinguishing among people of relatively equal merit. Those who oppose affirmative action because they prefer merit decisions in every case, might argue that yes, indeed, there is a resemblance here but all of the cases are wrong. Such people will therefore oppose tenure systems, seniority systems, and all other systems that give preference to anything other than merit. Still others might argue for disanalogies. Seniority, tenure, and veteran status base preferential decisions on something one has previous done (worked here a long time, published and taught effectively, served in the military), while racial status is something you are born with, not something you achieve through previous actions. This argument would probably exclude geographic diversity as well as race from the list of criteria that might lead to preferential treatment.

3. Most students find Brownmiller's analogy startling and clarifying. They think of porno houses in terms of sexual voyeurism, not hatred of women. Most students agree that they would picket a movie theater that featured anti-black or anti-semite propaganda. Why not, then, asks Brownmiller, picket a movie theater that features anti-female propaganda?

The analogy is powerful, as almost all students will agree. But on reflection, a number of disanalogies cloud this resemblance argument. Students will generally mention that pornographic films are made by paid performers, both women and men, who voluntarily choose this work and who--Linda Lovelace's protestations notwithstanding--often profess to enjoy their work and who see themselves as liberating people from Victorian taboos. There seem to be no parallel cases of Jewish or black actors who voluntarily produce Nazi-like racist propaganda. Apparently there is a kind of satisfaction that comes from pornography that is different from the satisfaction of racial propaganda. Another difference frequently mentioned is that racist propaganda seems overt; there is no doubt that racial hatred is the theme of the material. But pornography, to male students at least, does not seem overtly anti-female. It might be overtly anti-personal, or overtly anti-loving. But if it reduces persons to things, it seems to do so as much for men as for women. Finally, pornography and racial propaganda seem to arise from different regions of the psyche. Many male students will see pornography as one end of a spectrum that begins with mainstream advertising and t.v. shows; moves through PG-13 and then R-rated movies or through Cosmopolitan, Playboy and Penthouse magazines; then to soft pornography on cable TV or hotel "adult" channels; and finally to explicit hard core pornography. Mainstream pornography, male students will often claim, is neither sadistic nor perverse; it simply portrays explicitly the sexual activities hinted at elsewhere in the spectrum. If this is "anti-female" propaganda rooted in hatred of women, they will claim, it doesn't feel that way psychologically. When teenage boys hide Playboy under their mattresses, they are driven by newly discovered sexual desire--a longing for women, not a hatred of women. They don't hide under their mattresses anti-semite or anti-black propaganda. The presence of sexual desire in pornography is a complicating disanalogy that Brownmiller's argument doesn't adequately confront. For further analysis of Brownmiller's essay, see our discussion under the "Analysis of Readings" section of this Instructor's Manual.

Chapter 13

(p. 293) Answers will vary.

(p. 296) See our discussions of these arguments in the "Analysis of Readings" section of this Instructor's Manual.

Chapter 14

(pp. 317-318) Answers will vary.

(p. 322) See our discussion of these essays in the "Analysis of Readings" section of this Instructor's Manual.

Chapter 15

(p. 345) 1. If you stop terrorism, you will experience the following beneficial consequences: Rise in world respect, elimination of fear of retaliation, greater chance of success at the conference table, increased trade with Free World countries. 2. Terrorism is permitted if your actions are aimed at foreigners rather than at our native countrymen, if your actions are aimed at bettering the lives of our countrymen, and if the foreigners are clearly oppressive. You are urged to follow the Golden Rule when dealing with your fellow countrymen but to alter that rule when dealing with foreigners: Do unto foreigners as the foreigners have done unto you.

(p. 349) See our discussion of the Le Guin and the Levin essays in the "Analysis of Readings" section of this Instructor's Manual.

Chapter 16

(p. 378) This is a good exercise to teach use of the library. Dividing up the work among group members leads to a peer-teach-peer team approach to learning library skills. In our experience, this is a more effective approach than the traditional librarian-conducted tour of the library.

Chapter 17

(p. 385) Having students look closely at the differences between the summaries and the original can lead to productive learning. Students should particularly see how the differences between the two writers' purposes leads to somewhat different summaries with different focuses. Both of these summaries differ from data-dumps in that each writer's focus stays clearly on his or her own argument; material is extracted from the original not for its own sake but to support the writer's own point.

(p. 394) 1. Martha's passage is different from a data-dump because Martha selects research information purposefully to support her own meanings. 2. She uses Levin to increase the complexity of her own argument. Her essay opposes all forms and instances of terrorism. She wants to show how Levin's utilitarian support of torture cannot be extended to terrorism. She thus uses Levin to raise a complex question. 3. Point out to students how Martha has made slight changes from the original text within her brackets and has made omissions which she indicates with ellipses. 4. She keeps the focus on her own ideas.

(p. 396) This is an excellent exercise for clarifying what we mean by plagiarism in academia. Point out to students how Lucy's citation of the original material permits her to borrow ideas, but doesn't permit her to borrow language, which must be documented with quotation marks. By showing students where Lucy has copied word for word, you can stress the importance of writing in the student's own voice.

(p. 411) 1. and 2. We confess that we haven't checked out the sources used by these student writers, so we don't know what discussion might ensue. 3. Students should note that the APA system emphasizes date of research and downplays an author's individuality (initials only rather than full names). The implication here is that users of the APA system are scientists involved in cumulative, progressive research so that older research is of lesser value because it is out of date. In contrast, users of the MLA system, generally people in literature and related humanities, often refer to past studies that have an almost timeless quality. Dates are less important than the names of the scholars. Old essays by grand masters like Northrup Frye or William Empson may be of more value than a recent essay by an unknown. Thus full names are highlighted and date of publication is relegated to a later position in an MLA bibliographic entry.

Appendix One

(p. 433-434) 1. a. <u>Ad hominem</u>. The moral character of the arguer is here irrelevant to the logic of the argument. b. <u>false dilemma</u>. There may be other choices that the arguer doesn't consider. c. <u>Begging the question</u>: The person who doubts the claim (The bible is true) doubts it precisely because he doubts the reason (It is the inspired word of God). d. <u>Slippery slope</u>. Starting at point A on a slope does not mean we will necessarily slide all the way down to point G. e. Either <u>hasty generalization</u> or <u>post hoc ergo propter hoc</u>. Just because the tornadoes occurred after the A-bomb testing does not mean that the A-bomb testing caused the tornados. f. <u>Bandwagon appeal</u>. The fact that other nations have adopted socialized medicine does not mean that it is the best form of health care or that it is appropriate for the U.S. This could also be a <u>faulty analogy</u> in that conditions that make socialized medicine work in other countries might not obtain in the United States. (On the other hand, this could also be a very persuasive analogy, suggesting how hard it is to tell when a good argument slips into a fallacious one.) g. A reverse <u>ad hominem</u>? <u>Bandwagon</u>? <u>Appeal to false authority</u>? It is a bandwagon or false authority appeal to the extent that the person is swayed by the endorsement of Hollywood movie stars, who are not, after all, political experts. By claiming, however, that the movie stars have no self-interest in supporting liberal policies, the writer apparently believes he is strengthening the endorsement. It is difficult to know exactly what name to call this curious piece of misreasoning. h. <u>Circular argument</u>. Here the reason is merely a restatement of the claim in different language. i. <u>Hasty generalization</u>. No matter how much evidence is supplied about the two renters and the local homeowners, the observed sample is too small to warrant the sweeping conclusion. j. <u>False dilemma</u>. Maybe a third choice is possible.

2.a. In saying that America is not simply "a piece of dirt" but rather a certain set of principles, Clancy is leaving out a good deal of middle ground; in particular, he's ignoring principles that aren't friendly to the argument he's making but are still arguably identifiable as "American" principles. He's also leaving out all the institutions that have evolved out of those principles (including the military) and, arguably, departed from some of them along the way. This portion of the argument could, hence, qualify as a False Dilemma (that is, America is either a piece of dirt or it is the principles I am selectively emphasizing).

In turn, Clancy attributes all that's good about America and all its successes to the above-mentioned principles. This would appear to constitute a possible case of Post Hoc Ergo Propter Hoc in that other factors have certainly contributed as much or more to our successes (in particular abundant natural resources and an extremely late settlement period coincident with the rise of industrialism).

To argue that America's primary reason for going to war is to defend and promulgate a certain set of principles requires some highly selective hindsight. At the outset of the war with Iran, President Bush stressed to the public and argued to Congress, that "American interests" were in jeopardy. The same argument was made forcefully in Panama. Clearly national self-interest and protection of resources as well as principles motivate us to go to war.

In concluding that one can ask a Pole to prove that the principles we are heir to are "the only ones that work" (itself an evident Hasty Generalization in that many governments, blending elements of democracy, socialism, and even monarchy, appear to work reasonably well in spite of differences with our own), Clancy is setting up a case of False Authority. The average Pole will only know that the form of government used in his country did not work well.

Finally, in referring to these principles as the "distillation of 10,000 years of human social evolution," Clancy would seem to be overstating the case a bit. 10,000 years of human history have indeed passed, and at the end of that period we do have our principles. But to see the latter as a conscious result of the former remains unproven. Certainly socialism could make the same claim (indeed any alternative to monarchy could make the claim) but until we see how those principles result necessarily from that evolution, the argument remains tenuous.

2.b. In dismissing Congressman Mrazek's initiative to prevent logging in the Tongass National Forest by asserting that Mrazek "never saw a tree in his life," Mr. Young could, ostensibly, be justified in questioning Mrazek's authority. But since the statement is clearly untrue and since one could make an intelligent proposal about restricting logging without being an expert on trees, the remark constitutes an <u>ad hominem</u> argument. If one were to extend the logic of Young's remark, one would be in the precarious position of asserting that only physicians could propose health legislation and so on.

2.c. President Sarney's remark to Wirth is a clear case--and clear cases are hard to find--of "Appeal to Common Practice," better known in some circles as two-wrongs-make-a-right. Sarney's point is that if it's OK to log the Tongass, it's OK to log the Amazon Basin. Of course, such arguments have powerful roots in the doctrine of fairness. However wrong the practices may be, is it fair of us to demand restrictions of others we wouldn't put on ourselves? Some might also classify this as a case of False Analogy and argue that the Tongass is a quite different situation from the rain forests. From Sarney's perspective, though, the argument is an appeal to common practice (irrational premises) that requires further justification.

Appendix Two

(pp. 441-442) 1. Answers will vary. 2. According to social science research, all these assertions are true. What is important in this exercise, however, is for students to learn to interact in groups and to see how their group arrives at decisions.

(pp. 442-451): <u>A Several Days' Group Project: Defining "Good Argumentative Writing</u>." This group task is explained in detail in the text. Instructors might like to know, however, what teachers in our own programs have said about the four essays. Our evaluations, of course, should not be regarded as "correct answers."

"Bloody Ice"

This essay inevitably falls into the "B" range in our staff norming sessions. Most instructors praise it for its vivid opening and its relatively clear sense of structure as well as its transitions between paragraphs. People tend to fault it for the awkwardness of its language (e.g. "a tradition for survival" is a phrase that makes little sense), the abruptness of its transitions between sentences, and its logic. It is unclear just how the quotas set by the U.S. Seal Protection Act add up. Moreover, the writer suggests that "the seals are being killed off at an almost greater rate than they can remultiply" which would seem to be a level of zero population growth, not diminishment. (The confusion apparently hinges on the fact that the other factors mentioned combined with the seal killing result in declining populations.) Moreover, the student's second reason for opposing seal killing--that it's "inhumane"--needs considerable development by way of a definitional argument. Why is kicking a seal in the head less humane than clubbing? Moreover, the student's concluding proposal appears to skirt much of the ethical issue raised in the opening. Would a vivid description of domestic seal "harvesting" be any less repugnant to us?

"RSS Should Not Provide Dorm Room Carpets"

In its present state, this essay gets a "C" or "C-" from teachers in our programs, but its potential is much higher. The student writer herself was pleased with this draft because, as she reported, "it changed the minds of students in my group." The loss of opportunity to paint and decorate one's own room, the increased possibility of damage from spills, and the likelihood of higher room fees and forfeited damage deposits proved to be effective audience-based reasons opposing the installation of university-provided carpets.

But the draft is confusingly organized and underdeveloped. The end of the first paragraph predicts three parallel reasons (but note that lack of parallel structure in the last three sentences of the introduction confuses the writer's intention). The body of the essay, however, maps two reasons (reason three, as predicted in the introduction, gets collapsed into reason two). Most readers get confused in the transition from Trish's blueberry pie to the carpet issue and get more confused when Trish returns in paragraph two. Paragraph two is especially confusing because it opens by summarizing and refuting opposing views when the mapping and transitions led the reader to anticipate development of the first reason. Despite the length of the paragraph, the writer provides few grounds to support the reason "many students don't want carpets." Similarly, reason two could be strengthened with more financial data. Readers aren't quite sure how to interpret $300 per room. How many total rooms would be carpeted? What is the total figure for carpeting? How large a figure is that comparatively in terms of the total budget for maintenance or capital improvement? Where would that money come from? Would student room rates really skyrocket? In short, by clarifying the organization of the essay and by providing more factual grounds, this writer could improve the argument dramatically.

"The Sterling Hall Dorm Food"

Most composition teachers have encountered a few "bad dorm food" snoozers, but this one--to us--seems worse than usual. We give it an "F." The dominant problem is that the writer has invented his grounds--the hypothetical case of Johnny who pays too much for lousy food and finds a hair in his burrito to boot. An attack on dorm food, we tell students, is serious business. Managers and cooks and food buyers make their living running cafeterias and stand to lose their livelihoods if the charges against them are well grounded. It is dishonest to make up your data. (Such is the mini-sermon we give our students.) Additionally, the essay is organized chronologically rather than hierarchically. Instead of reasons supported by evidence, we get the narrative of Johnny as he progresses through the cafeteria. Nor are the narrative details consistent. Sometimes Johnny is a struggling poor student trying to make ends meet, yet he still has a Giorgio wallet. The writer needs to start over.

"ROTC Courses Should Not Get College Credit"

Students almost always cite this essay as the best of the group. So do we. We give it an "A" as an example of good freshman writing. The writer's three reasons are clearly stated and differentiated from each other: (1) ROTC courses do not stress inquiry and true questioning. (2) ROTC courses are not academically strenuous and thus inflate the GPAs of ROTC students. (3) ROTC classes keep students from taking more valuable liberal arts courses. One of the strengths of this essay--worth pointing out to students--is the way it emphasizes both grounds and warrants. Note, for example, the copious grounds provided for reason number one--the need of officers to follow orders, the difference between ROTC and other courses in frequency of in-class debates, the testimony of the writer's uncle from Vietnam days, and the similarity of the uncle's experience with the writer's own during the Kuwait crisis. But as he cites these grounds, he simultaneously focuses the reader's attention on the warrant--the value of critical thinking and open questioning as emphasized in his other courses. Another strength of this essay is its proposal conclusion. Rather than arguing for the abolition of ROTC--the writer clearly values being a cadet--the writer proposes that ROTC training be considered an extra-curricular activity like athletics.

Supporters of ROTC as an academic field might raise numerous objections to this paper. At the level of grounds, they might claim that ROTC provides more room for intellectual debate than the writer acknowledges or that the writer doesn't provide hard data on grade distribution in ROTC courses. Similarly, they might object to some of his examples as biased and unrepresentative. Or they might question the writer's warrants: Should ROTC be an inquiry and debate course--like literature or political science, say--or is it more like a science and engineering course, where, presumably, great policy debates are also infrequent? There is plenty to praise here, but clearly only one side of the issue is represented.

"Legalization of Prostitution?"

This is a tricky one. Our students tend to like this essay. Sometimes, in fact, they rate it second behind the ROTC argument. Most English teachers rate it low, although occasionally some will give it high marks. Clearly there are strengths in this essay intermixed with glaring weaknesses. The authors of this text give it a "D." The overriding weakness we find in the paper is the writer's lack of control over organization, leading to a circular repetition of generalizations and an almost total absence of grounds. The second paragraph ends with a clear enough claim accompanied by four parallel because clauses as reasons. This claim, however, doesn't emerge coherently from an introduction that raises the issue question and sets the parameters of the debate. She could begin, for example, with a review of the controversy over legalization of prostitution or, alternatively, with an exposition of the problem that she proposes to solve. But it is not clear that she is doing either. When the writer states (in paragraph 2) that "crime rates are soaring, diseases are spreading wildly, and the environment on the streets is rapidly decaying," it is not clear whether she is talking about crime and disease among prostitutes, among the people who associate with prostitutes, or among the population in general. Nor is it clear what she means by "environment." The reader isn't quite sure whether the writer is concerned with the plight of prostitutes or the plight of society.

The organization of the paper is confusing since the writer sets up expectations which aren't met. The body of the paper seems to follow the chronological order of objections made by opponents rather than the order predicted in the thesis. The thesis predicts the following order: legalization of prostitution would (1) reduce the wave of epidemics, (2) decrease high crime rates, (3) provide revenue, and (4) get the girls off the streets where sexual crimes often occur (although it isn't clear how the last reason differs from the second reason). The actual order of paragraphs is quite different: (1) reduction of epidemics; (2) increase of business revenues; and (3) discussion of the morality of the issue. In none of these paragraphs, however, does the writer bring data to bear on a reason--e.g., data about epidemics, facts and figures about prostitution as a business, and so forth (lack of research? problems seeing how to use data?)

Part of the writer's problem seems to be a kind of psychological preoccupation with her readers' moral objections. She imagines her reader saying, "But if you legalize prostitution aren't you saying that it is morally OK?" To which she replies: "It exists; its the oldest profession; it's reality; if we say it is the root of all evil, it still won't go away; who's to say whether it is right or wrong?" and so forth. She needs to consolidate her discussion of the moral issue into one section--perhaps the introduction or conclusion--and use the rest of the space to develop her cost/benefit analysis with research data. The plan presented in her thesis and because clauses seems workable. For a rewrite, she might be encouraged to stick to that plan, fleshing out each section with grounds.

III. CRITERIA CHECKLISTS FOR EVALUATING DRAFTS

In this section of the Instructor's Manual we provide a variety of checklists that instructors can duplicate for students' use during draft review workshops. Some teachers may prefer simply to adapt for this purpose the "Questions for Analyzing Individual Arguments," appearing on p. 455 of the text. Others may wish to resort to a more general checklist such as the one provided below. [Note: This checklist has been slightly adapted from the one that originally appeared in earlier editions of the text but does not appear in the fourth edition. As we claimed in earlier editions, in addition to its value for the peer reviewing of drafts, this checklist serves as a selective summary of important points and concepts from the first eight chapters of the text.]

GENERAL CHECKLIST FOR EVALUATING DRAFTS

Understanding the Writer's Intentions
- Create a "says" and a "does" statement for each paragraph of the draft.
- What issue is being addressed in this draft? Try to represent it in the form of an issue-question.
- What is the writer's thesis (claim, proposition)?
- How would you summarize the writer's main reasons as because clauses?
- Construct a tree diagram, flow chart, or outline of the writer's argument.
- Is the draft a one-sided or multi-sided argument?
- What audience does the writer address? The opposition? Neutral third party? Fellow believers? Others?
- What stance does the writer take toward opposing views? Tough-minded and combative? Conciliatory? Other?
- Summarize the writer's argument in 100-200 words. (If you have trouble summarizing the argument, discuss difficulties with the writer. Have him or her talk you through the argument orally and then make recommendations for revision.)

Critiquing the Writer's Argument
- How effective are the writer's supporting reasons? Are there any additional reasons the writer might use?
- Is each reason supported with effective grounds in the form of factual data, evidence, statistics, testimony, or appropriate chains of reasons? Identify any reasons you find to be weak.
- Do the warrants for any of the reasons need to be explictly articulated and supported with backing?
- To what extent are the supporting reasons audience-based instead of writer-based? Do each of the supporting enthymemes rest in values shared by the audience?
- Does the writer attend adequately to opposing views? As a reviewer of this draft, how would you go about refuting the writer's argument?
- If the writer summarizes opposing views, does he or she follow the principle of charity by providing a fair, accurate, complete summary that makes an opposition's "best case" or that represents the multiple voices in the conversation?
- If the writer rebuts opposing views, is the rebuttal clear and effective? How could it be improved?
- Does the writer project an effective ethos? If not, what might he or she do to strengthen it?
- Does the writer make effective use of pathos? How could appeals to pathos be strengthened through narratives, images and details, metaphor and analogy, or word choice?

Critiquing the Draft's Readability
- Identify any places in the draft that are confusing or unclear.
- Has the writer used and documented his or her sources accurately and appropriately? Alert the writer to any problems in the use of sources that you detect (see Chapter 17).
- Alert the writer if the effectiveness of the essay appears to be diminished by wordiness, clumsy sentence structure, or any other grammatical or mechanical problems.

Summary of Peer Reviewer's Recommendations
- What are the major strengths of this draft?
- What are the major weaknesses?
- What suggestions can you offer the writer for eliminating the weaknesses?

CHECKLISTS FOR THE FIVE STASES OF ARGUMENTS

The following checklists are intended to supplement the "General Checklist for Evaluating Drafts" provided above by referring specifically to the specialized claim types discussed in the stases chapters, Chapters 10-15. Each is preceded by a brief summary for teachers of key points in the chapter.

DEFINITION ARGUMENTS (Chapter 10)

Probably the greatest difficulty students face in constructing definitional arguments is the demand for abstract thinking. While the "match" portion of a "criteria-match" definitional argument may be pretty straightforward, the development of criteria is much trickier. Forming criteria forces students to examine relationships among concepts and to fashion subtle distinctions. It's especially important in this regard that they come up with boundary cases which really do test the adequacy of their criteria. We should note too that we are not entirely sanguine about the use of the traditional Aristotelian mode of definition here. Obviously, it is at odds with a good deal of contemporary semantic theory and some of our own beliefs about language. On the other hand, it appears to be the best place for students to begin to understand some of the complexities of definition and prepares them also to comprehend what's at stake in contemporary critiques of "essentialist" language theory.

Supplemental Checklist for Definitional Claims
- Are both the criteria and the match at issue in the definitional argument? If not, which one is at stake?
- Has the writer specified the criteria for the definition?
- Which of the criteria cited are "necessary" to labelling something "Y"? Can you think of any cases in which something lacking one of these criteria would still qualify as a Y? Can you think of another criterion unmentioned by the writer which in your view is necessary for something to be a "Y"?
- Does the writer specify criteria which if met are "sufficient" to call something "Y"? Can you think of any examples of things which possess these criteria and still don't qualify as "Y"?

- How does the term at issue match up with these criteria?
- Are the examples cited for how something is or is not a Y representative, or are they too narrow or too extreme? Can you think of other examples in which the thing in question does not meet the criteria?
- Has the "rule of justice" (that all beings in the same essential category be treated in the same way) been violated in any way?
- Does the writer acknowledge counter-arguments and effectively refute them?

CAUSE/CONSEQUENCE ARGUMENTS (Chapter 11)

Beyond the tendency of writers to oversimplify causality, to mistake immediate causes for "The Cause," and to pronounce causality where only correlation is established, the foremost difficulty of causal arguing is the tendency to rush to judgment. That is, most causal arguments lead to evaluative conclusions. They establish that person X or Y is guilty and should be punished or that substance A or B is responsible and should deleted. Too often, student writers fail to create a framework for such an argument whereby the connection between causality and evaluation is clear. Too often, the causal argument is slighted and the writer leaps to evaluation of consequences, particularly if the consequences are negative.

Supplemental Checklist for Causal Claims

- Does the causal argument presented here deal with a specific, one-time-only event or phenomenon or does it deal with a recurrent event or phenomenon?
- If it deals with a one-time occurrence, does the writer establish a clear causal chain (or chains) with no crucial missing links? Does the writer make clear in the process of describing this chain just <u>how</u> the causal mechanism works?
- If it deals with a recurrent phenomenon, does the writer show that the same or similar results repeatedly follow from the alleged cause(s)? Does the writer explain <u>how</u> the causal mechanism works? Can you think of any exceptions to the correlation established?
- If the writer has established a clear correlation between two or more phenomena, has he also established clearly the direction of the cause? Has he ruled out the possibility that some unnamed factor might account for the correlation?

- Does the writer offer evidence from scientific experimentation? If so, do the data appear to be accurate and representative? Can you think of any important variables which haven't been controlled for? Who conducted the scientific study? Might they have an interest in the outcome of the study?
- Has the writer used an analogy argument to establish a plausible causal linkage? What disanalogies can you think of between the cited phenomenon/event and the one at issue?
- Has the writer properly weighted the causal factors, or has he or she given too much weight to a causal factor that is simply one of many? What causal factors might be more important than the one(s) focused on by the writer?

RESEMBLANCE ARGUMENTS (Chapter 12)

We focus throughout this chapter on the care that writers must exercise in limiting the force of their resemblance claims. Such claims are indeed seductive for readers and writers alike, and it's all too easy to take them literally. What we don't discuss, however, is just how difficult it is for most of us to produce even faulty resemblances. Most students will need a lot of time and practice at developing analogies before they're ready to incorporate them confidently into an argument. (Some, of course, will take to it quite naturally, thus further discouraging their classmates.) Most will need some practice with analogy-making. We thus encourage you to let them play with random combinations of items so they can come to see that analogies are fabrications and that it's OK to fool around with the "Natural Order of Things." Addictive behavior may on the surface have nothing to do with defense spending, but a good writer can always produce a meaningful connection.

Supplemental Checklist for Resemblance Claims
- What is being compared to what? Which of the two terms of the comparison is at issue (the tenor) and which serves as the vehicle for clarifying or commenting on the term at issue? Are you as reader familiar enough with the second term (the "vehicle") that the comparison is understandable and persuasive?
- List all pertinent points of comparison that the writer has made in the argument. What is the most important point of

comparison and why? What is the least important point of comparison and why?
- Are any of the points of comparison "strained" or sufficiently irrelevant that they should be left out? Are any pertinent points of comparison left out?
- Has the writer been sufficiently careful about qualifying the comparison? If not, is the writer's purpose to shock an audience into some sort of recognition about the term at issue?
- What are the major dissimilarities ("disanalogies") between the two terms? If a precedence argument, what circumstances might be different from one case to the next?
- Think of at least one counter-analogy that might cause an audience to reach a different conclusion than the one suggested by the writer's comparison. If a precedence argument, think of another precedent that suggests a different conclusion from the one suggested by the writer's comparison.

EVALUATION ARGUMENTS (Chapter 13)

A perennial difficulty for writers defending evaluation claims is to get beyond personal, largely unconscious values in order to consider the item being evaluated from the point of view of its purpose and function. More subtly, they will sometimes evaluate an item from the perspective of the one purpose that most affects them, no matter how peripheral that purpose is to the item under scrutiny. Both difficulties, or course, are related to the persistent belief that all evaluative judgments are "subjective" anyway. In teaching evaluation arguments, therefore, instructors should help students discover criteria for judgment that writer and reader are likely to share.

Supplemental Checklist for Evaluation Claims
- What is the writer evaluating? (What is the X term?) What category does the writer place X in (the Y term)? Is this the smallest relevant class in which X might be placed?
- What does the writer see as the primary functions of the class? Does he ignore any significant functions of this class? Does the writer cite any functions which seem peripheral or irrelevant to the class? Does the writer discriminate between more and less significant functions/purposes of the class?

- Are the criteria for judging X clearly related to the functions/ purposes of the class to which it belongs? Are the criteria weighted in accordance with the extent to which they allow X to realize the purposes of its class? Does the writer ignore any appropriate criteria that X clearly doesn't meet?
- What evidence does the writer present that X meets the established criteria?
- How does the writer measure the extent to which X meets a given criterion? How trustworthy in your view are these measures? Are the measures significantly narrower than the criteria would suggest?
- Are the criteria based on what's normal for members of X's class or what's ideal or a mixture of both?
- Are there any mitigating circumstances which might cause you to apply the criteria to X in a less strict manner?
- Does the writer's evaluation take the cost of X into account?

PROPOSAL ARGUMENTS (Chapter 14)

Perhaps the hardest thing to get students to do when fashioning a proposal argument is to account for the costs of their proposal. It's human nature to ignore or downplay such costs. For this reason, group work--getting other students to articulate potential costs for the writer--is crucial here. Equally important, of course, is to convince readers that a problem truly exists and to create persuasive reasons to act on the proposal.

Supplemental Checklist for Proposal Claims
- What is the problem that needs to be addressed?
- Does the writer show why it is a significant problem? Does the writer give "presence" to the problem? Does the writer make clear just <u>how</u> negative consequences will arise if the proposal is not initiated?
- Does the writer persuade you that the problem is a soluble one and not simply "in the nature of things"?
- Does the writer make clear just <u>how</u> the proposal will solve the problem? Are any significant aspects of the problem left unaddressed by the proposal? Does the writer show how the proposal will be paid for?
- What are the benefits of enacting the proposal? Does the proposal address the needs/interests of the audience being addressed by the proposal?

- Does the writer take into account any possible alternative proposals which offer better/cheaper solutions?
- Does the writer face up to potential negative consequences of enacting the proposal such as inequitable distribution of costs, possible ecological damage, and so forth?

ETHICAL ARGUMENTS (Chapter 15)

Writing ethical arguments can be both intellectually daunting and emotionally strenuous for many students. Without the guiding light of a "class purpose" to illuminate their evaluation, it's easy to fall into confusion. "The Good," as opposed to "a good X," is a maddeningly complex notion. In turn, submitting some of their most deeply held beliefs up for rational scrutiny may cause many to squirm. We have found that a brief introduction to principle-based versus consequence-based ethical theories gives students a good start toward a more thoughtful analysis of their own ethical decisions.

Supplemental Checklist for Ethical Claims

- Is the argument based on some enduring principle, on the consequences of the ethical choice, or on some combination?
- If the argument is based on some principle, does that principle specifically enjoin or prohibit the action or does it offer "ideal case" guidelines that must be interpreted for the given situation?
- Could someone reasonably interpret that principle in such a way as to reach a different conclusion? Do you know of any other principles possessed of the same degree of universality which enjoin a different response?
- What negative consequences will follow from the decision based on principle?
- If the argument is based on consequences, what evidence does the writer offer that the anticipated consequences will in fact come to pass?
- Does the writer clearly divide those consequences into costs and benefits and demonstrate that the benefits of the decision will outweigh the costs?
- Does the decision based on consequence violate any universal, or at least commonly accepted, ethical principle?
- Is the writer's decision capable of being "universalized," that is, treated as a precedent for future decisions of a similar nature?

IV. ANALYSIS OF THE READINGS THROUGHOUT THE TEXT

In this section of the Instructor's Manual, we provide close analyses of the readings throughout the text. Our intention is to help instructors regard the readings not so much as "models for students to emulate" but as "contributions to a conversation," full of strengths and weaknesses. Our analyses should help instructors initiate class discussion of any of the readings, armed with a sense of each essay's vulnerable points and corresponding points of rhetorical strength. Of course, many instructor's analyses of a given reading may differ considerably from our own.

ESSAYS FROM CHAPTER 10 (DEFINITION)

• **Kathy Sullivan, "Oncore, Obscenity, and the Liquor Control Board" (pp. 220-221)**

Student writer Kathy Sullivan claims that a series of photographs displayed at a Seattle gay bar should not be considered "obscene." The Washington State Liquor Control Board had enjoined the owner of the bar from displaying the photographs on the grounds that they portrayed male genitalia. Sullivan uses criteria derived from legal dictionaries to oppose the liquor board's decision. From Black's Law Dictionary, Sullivan derives three criteria that, if met, would make the photographs obscene: (1) The dominant theme of the photographs, when judged by the average person applying "contemporary community standards," must appeal primarily to "prurient interest. (2) The material must be pornographic in a hard core sense or at least go beyond customary limits in candor and representation. And (3) it must be utterly without redeeming social purpose. She also adds a fourth criterion from Pember's Mass Media Law: If there is a chance that the material will be viewed by children, then the standards for obscenity are much tighter.

Sullivan argues that the photographs do not meet any of the criteria. She begins by arguing that the relevant community standards should be those of the homosexual community, not the general community, since this bar is patronized predominantly by gays. Based on this view of community standards, she argues that the material has a redeeming social purpose--that of promoting safe sex--and that this purpose, rather than prurient interest, is the dominant appeal of the photographs. Further she argues that since the photographs do not depict sexual acts, but simply show male nudity, they are not pornographic. Finally, she argues that the location of the photographs in a gay bar means that children will not see them.

It is difficult to evaluate Sullivan's argument without being able to see the photographs first hand. Because she doesn't describe them in detail, it is difficult to tell how the theme of "safe sex" is portrayed in the photographs. Does the fact that patrons pulled off the bandaids covering "private parts" indicate prurient interest or just good humor? That the State Liquor Control Board complained only of male nudity, rather than of homosexual orientation or explicit sexual acts, suggests that these photographs are tamer than the more famous Mapplethorpe photographs involved in the NEH controversy.

Perhaps the most vulnerable part of her argument is her restriction of contemporary community standards to those of the homosexual community. Skeptics might have several problems with this argument. First, it isn't clear that there is a legal precedent for this kind of narrowing of community standards. The courts may have intended to let the citizens of, say, Des Moines, Iowa, set their standards for obscenity differently from those of New York City. It is not clear, however, that they intended standards to vary from one side of the street to another. Such narrowing might lead to an anarchic splintering of large communities into sub-communities. Should the standards for obscenity in a working class bar on the waterfront differ from those of an upscale bar in the banking district?

Her narrowing of "community" also leads to a double standard that leaves unchallenged the values of the larger community. Should art with homosexual themes be restricted to homosexual establishments and therefore banned from places where heterosexuals gather? Sullivan seems to take this position. The larger issues of whether it is just for a society to be permissive about female nudity but not male nudity or to endorse heterosexual eros (in advertising, say) but not homosexual eros are not addressed. Some readers might have wished to see Sullivan tackle these larger issues, rather than finesse them by limiting the relevant standards to those of the homosexual community.

- Charles Krauthammer, "How to Save the Homeless Mentally Ill" (pp. 221-227)

Krauthammer's argument begins with the widely publicized case of Joyce Brown, the homeless person who, contending that she was a street person by choice, refused New York City's attempts to help her. It's the sort of hard case that makes for bad law insofar as it represents an irresolvable clash between society's respect for the autonomous individual and society's obligation to care for those who can't care for themselves. Krauthammer's contention is that in the case of the mentally ill homeless at least, the obligation of society to provide for the destitute should take precedence over its obligation to recognize individual freedoms. What sort of freedom is it after all, Krauthammer asks, other than a freedom to suffer? Indeed, Krauthammer's major reason for promoting institutionalization for the homeless is that "the city, with its army of grate-dwellers, is a school for callousness." For Krauthammer, the spectacle of suffering that must be ignored contributes to a climate of moral insensitivity that hampers the sense of community essential to a civilized society. Thus, he considerably broadens the grounds for institutionalization, requiring only that the mentally ill be living in a "degraded" state, not that they pose an immediate danger to themselves or to others.

So, the first stage of Krauthammer's argument is essentially a definitional claim: "In the end, the Brown case boils down to a problem of category, not a problem of principle. Is she a schizophrenic or a hobo?" If she's a schizophrenic, and thereby living in a "degraded" state, she needs to be institutionalized. The definition issue then leads to the second part of his argument, which is a proposal to build a network of asylums to which the homeless mentally ill might be committed. Based on preliminary results from New York's project HELP, Krauthammer believes such a treatment program can be successful. Unfortunately, in lieu of any conclusive data on the numbers of homeless mentally ill or the costs of maintaining such institutions, it's not clear how much Krauthammer's proposal might cost. While capping the mortgage deduction at $20,000/year would yield $1 billion, it's not clear that Congress would ever approve such a politically unpopular move. (Though to be sure, it does seem an appropriate place to look for money for the homeless.) At issue, as can be seen in student writer Stephen Bean's essay later in the text (pp. 330-338), are whether mental institutions (as opposed to community care) are the best places to treat mentally ill persons, whether the poverty of mentally ill persons is primarily a medical or a socio-economic problem, and whether pumping money into asylum-based mental health care is the best way for society to spend its dollars in the fight to end homelessness. By not raising these issues, Krauthammer keeps his argument largely one-sided.

ESSAYS FROM CHAPTER 11 (CAUSE/CONSEQUENCE)

- Carl Sagan, "Warming of the World" (pp. 253-257)

Since this essay's causal linkage is detailed in the middle of the chapter, we will spend little time on it here. What distinguishes Sagan's essay is the clarity of his explanation for a complex causal mechanism. Note how carefully Sagan builds up to the importance of CO_2 in explaining how the earth's atmosphere controls climate. Note in turn how he makes clear through illustration that an apparently small rise in temperature can have enormous effects on our environment.

Like all one-time occurrences, the Greenhouse Effect is open to certain sorts of question. In particular, Sagan shows clearly how the causal mechanism works, but can't prove beyond a doubt that it will continue to operate in the prescribed manner into the indefinite future. We have no historical data which show us precisely how the scenario will work itself out. And given that the build up in CO_2 will bring about a multitude of changes in the earth's atmosphere, some of which surely can't be anticipated, it seems possible that anticipated effects might be either countered or accelerated by unanticipated ones. Sagan's argument, then, suffers from the necessary tentativeness that attends any sort of projection of a complex, one-time occurrence into the future. And the more complex the phenomenon, the more difficult the projection. Like so many scientific arguments in recent years, Sagan's argument is shadowed by the possibility that change occurs in a non-evolutionary, "catastrophic" fashion, whereby a threshold condition is achieved incrementally over a relatively long time and then suddenly great change is effected in an instant.

Sagan deals with these difficulties masterfully by keeping the focus on the causal mechanism itself (which is well understood) and the suggestive historical data that he does have available. Moreover, to impart greater urgency to his final proposal, he also underscores the darker side of the unknown possibilities. While the proposal suffers from a certain amount of vagueness, it appears generally reasonable in the context of the undeniably grim consequences he so convincingly sketches.

- Victor Fuchs, "Why Married Women Work" (pp. 259-262)

Fuchs' causal argument is paradigmatic in the way it first sets out a good "why" question--"Why do so many more married mothers work today than did in 1951?"; then demonstrates graphically the truth of the assertion implied by the question--by featuring a graph showing the steep climb in rates of working mothers; and finally considers a number of alternative explanations in turn until coming up with the best one.

He considers first the "feminist" explanation, that ties the increased number of women in the labor force to increased acceptance of feminist values; the trouble with this explanation is that it doesn't correlate temporally with the advancement of feminism. The rise in numbers of working mothers has gone on since 1950 while the feminist movement doesn't pick up steam until the mid-sixties. Moreover, there is no "sudden acceleration" in the rates of working mothers associated with the sudden acceleration of feminist ideas during this period; the rise is pretty steady for forty years.

He next considers the rising divorce rate as a cause. But while the accelerated divorce rate correlates with the acceleration of feminism, neither seems to have an effect on the steady rise in numbers of working mothers. And as for affirmative action, it too postdates the rise in working mothers, and also the patterns of employment don't follow the suggested pattern of affirmative action employment. (That is, women moved into more prestigious jobs at a much faster rate from 1950 to 1965 than they did between '65 and '79.)

The "economic necessity argument" (everyone today needs two paychecks to survive) doesn't square with economic data that suggest male breadwinners' real income rose significantly during the period being analyzed. (Fuchs doesn't consider here in any detail the notion that the definition of "necessity" has changed dramatically over time. Many families now claim, for example, to "need" second cars and homes and CD players. As the overall standard of living rises, the bottom of that standard--bare necessities--rises accordingly; hence the gap between a male's real income and "necessary" level may indeed grow even as the former rises. In saying that one can't explain a variable [the increase in working mothers] with a constant [need], Fuchs gives short shrift to the definitional claim that "need" is psychologically, not economically, defined and hence capable of fluctuation.)

Finally, Fuchs rejects the "time-saving devices" argument that suggests that women now have more time to enter the workforce because time spent on housework has been so dramatically cut by modern appliances and a streamlined marketing system. This is a classic case of mistaking effect for cause in Fuchs' eyes. As the value of time increases, we are willing to expend more on time-saving devices, thus making a market for them. He concludes with his "winners": higher wages and, more importantly, the shift to a service economy. The first cause is suggested by data showing that the likelihood of mothers working goes up sharply relative to their earning power (just as that likelihood drops as husband's earning power rises).

The second cause, the more surprising one (and it is the unexpectedness of the cause that makes it a significant argument), is that numbers of women working correlates with the shift in the economy from a manufacturing to a service economy. Here, he makes his claim plausible by suggesting that service jobs put no premium on physical strength, have flexible hours and allow more readily for part-time workers, and are typically located in residential areas. Further, Fuchs rejects the notion that the service industry has grown in response to the needs of the two paycheck family, suggesting instead that the dramatic increase in output per worker in the manufacturing fields makes service industries possible.

In evaluating Fuchs' argument, we need to keep in mind that while he makes a strong case for the "major" causes of mothers working, the rejected causes, including increased control over fertility, are undoubtedly contributing causes as well.

- **Mary Lou Torpey, "What Drugs I Take is None of Your Business" (pp. 257-258)**

One of the most refreshing aspects of this student essay, in contrast to Fuchs' essay, is the degree of personal involvement of the writer. While Fuchs establishes the issue in terms of statistics and general trends, Torpey keeps the focus on her own situation. The strength of this essay lies in the writer's ability to get her reader to experience with her some of the consequences of mandatory drug testing and in her pointing up two seldom considered consequences--the effect of testing on legitimate drug users and the way that public concern can render some drugs less accessible to legitimate users.

In challenging Torpey's position, perhaps the most interesting place to start is with her assumption that employers should not be privy to employees' medical histories. Should an employer not be allowed to give preference to workers with no history of medical problems? Is it "discrimination" if the disability has the potential to adversely affect performance? Moreover, since most employment application forms ask for medical information of various sorts, would Torpey be willing to say that someone in her position is justified in lying on such forms? If an employee with a medical history of epilepsy fails to tell an employer, is the employer liable for any on-the-job injuries suffered as a result of a seizure? Further, she draws no distinction between different sorts of jobs in her arguments against drug testing. While a teacher, clerk or secretary would seem to have a reasonable case against the drug testers, what about airline pilots, truck and bus drivers, and air traffic controllers? How does one balance the individuals' right to privacy against the public's right to safety?

- **Walter Minot, "Students Who Push Burgers" (pp. 262-263)**

Minot's argument is extremely informal, more in the way of alerting us to a plausible yet novel explanation for a much discussed phenomenon than it is a definitive argument. Drugs and TV don't account for lapses in student achievement, argues Minot; students aren't doing as well because they work too many hours per week outside of school. (Note here that Minot assumes diminished performance of today's students, which you may wish at least to question.)

The primary reason students work outside of school, according to Minot, is to pay for their cars. The primary reason they need a car is to get to work. Which is to say, the "economic necessity" argument touched on by Fuchs here gets a new twist--the variable and circular definition of necessity driving (literally) students to the marketplace. Minot's argument invariably produces reflective class discussion. Do jobs really teach teenagers the value of a dollar, as teenagers assert? Or do they distort a teenager's view of economic reality by providing spending money for luxuries while parents pick up the tab for essentials? Most teachers--in our experience--agree with Minot. Today's students are too busy working to devote themselves to studies; and seeing themselves as "workers," they also want to take their weekends off. This essay provides a good opportunity for reflection both on values and on causal mechanisms.

ESSAYS FROM CHAPTER 12 (RESEMBLANCE)

- Susan Brownmiller, "Against Our Will: Men, Women and Rape" (pp. 278-280)

Brownmiller's rhetorical problem, defined at the outset of her essay, is that the lines of the debate about pornography have been misdrawn. Because conservatives have taken the lead in the antipornography movement, feminist opponents of porn have had difficulty staking out a position on the issue. They must identify warrants for their claim that pornography is bad that won't be readily confused with conservative arguments and thereby alienate liberal allies who have traditionally taken a laissez faire attitude toward porn or who have defended it on First Amendment grounds.

Because she is breaking new ground on the topic and has to overcome some of her audience's most basic assumptions about the terms of the debate, it is hardly surprising that Brownmiller uses resemblances to help move her readers from familiar into unfamiliar territory. Her first major analogy is between women in pornographic films and playthings, "adult toys to be used, abused, broken and discarded."

If her audience accepts that equation, and the concomitant assumption that the thrill of pornography lies in the dehumanization of the women depicted in it rather than in pure sexual desire, Brownmiller's move from pornography to rape is fairly straightforward. Both porn and rape are essentially male inventions and expressions of violence toward and control of women.

At this point in the argument, Brownmiller shifts to two traditional liberal causes, anti-defamation and anti-violence, and asks her liberal readers how they can oppose racism and violence at the same time they allow pornography to flourish. In the case of racism, our intolerance for ethnic jokes and propaganda is contrasted to our tolerance for sleazy bookstores and theaters. If those same theaters depicted violence against Jews and blacks instead of against women, Brownmiller asks, would the ACLU still defend them so avidly? By the same token, how can we oppose violence on TV at the same time violence in pornography is allowed to flourish?

Like all resemblances, the ones cited by Brownmiller give a immediate presence to her position. Like all resemblances, they are more suggestive than decisive. While some pornographic films (e.g. the so called "snuff films") certainly are as odious as films "depicting the sadistic pleasures of gassing Jews or lynching blacks," most are not. And equation of pornographic violence to violence on TV breaks down on the accessibility issue (i.e. it's much easier to limit children's access to porn theaters than to limit their access to violence on network TV). Still, there are enough similarities in her resemblance claims to make her targeted audience squirm.

ESSAYS FROM CHAPTER 13 (EVALUATION)

- **Murray Weidenbaum, "How to Reform the Federal Tax System: Just the Basics, Please" (pp. 297-298)**

As an example of an evaluation argument, Weidenbaum's essay offers students an interesting approach, for what the writer says here appears motivated more by an effort to inform his audience than any genuine desire to persuade them. In fact, by virtue of the absence of clear reasons and supporting evidence, it comes close to exemplifying the kind of implicit argument (as opposed to an explicit argument) that we describe in Chapter 1. Granted the writer asserts a definite claim that might be expressed in this way: Any new tax system should fulfill six criteria if it is to obtain the support of a majority of taxpayers. Granted, the promotion of criteria for evaluating new tax systems ostensibly renders Weidenbaum's piece an evaluation argument. Still, apart from enumerating and explaining the various criteria, the writer seems to make little attempt to actually defend their legitimacy or to create an argument for their appropriateness, except to note that they are the product of "extended discussions with groups ranging from technical experts to ordinary taxpayers" (paragraph 4).

In discussing this essay, then, students should be encouraged to account for and evaluate the consequences of the absence of supporting evidence, considering such possibilities as these: is Weideman's audience such that he knows that he may count on them to "fill in the blanks" on their own? Does he know his audience to be particularly sympathetic to his point of view? Are the criteria such that they may be anticipated to be acceptable to anyone? What are the underlying assumptions behind these criteria? (Would anyone seriously take issue, for example, with the notion that the new tax system should be fair to the average taxpayer, or be understandable to the average citizen?) Does the absence of support for the writer's criteria finally discourage a reader from accepting his claim?

- Terry Tang, "Clinton Can Show Courage by Vetoing Bad Welfare Bill" (pp. 298-299)

What makes Tang's article an evaluation argument is his effort to persuade an audience that the latest welfare plan passed by Congress is ultimately a bad bill, for to do so, he must present reasons that match characteristics of the plan to a set of criteria defining bad bills. To that end, he maintains the plan is bad 1) because it saves money by denying welfare benefits to legal, tax-paying immigrants; 2) because it saves money by cutting funding specifically from food programs that serve children; 3) because it does not provide adequate funding for the job training and education necessary to prepare those to be deprived of benefits at the end of five years to find jobs; and 4) the repeal of welfare benefits at the end of five years is motivated by efforts not to foster recipients' self-sufficiency but rather to reduce federal spending.

It's worth pointing out that the writer takes few pains to argue the criteria by which the bill is judged to be bad; the writer assumes, for example, that the audience will share the underlying belief that any bill passed by representatives of a "nation of immigrants" that does not provide legal, tax-paying immigrants with the same benefits as its citizens is necessarily a bad bill; likewise any bill motivated by an effort to reduce federal spending. Again, students may be invited to consider the reason why the writer chooses not to argue his warrants, looking first to the context in which the article originally appeared, and the consequences.

- **Sam Isaacson, "Would Legalization of Gay Marriage Be Good for the Gay Community?" (pp. 300-302)**

Students looking for a model essay responding to the major writing assignment included on p. 283 in this chapter will recognize the virtues of Isaacson's essay in this context immediately. As the assignment directs, Isaacson takes as the issue a genuinely controversial one, which he represents in the form of the question that serves as the title of his essay: would legalizing gay marriage be good for gays? Thus, the legalization of gay marriage becomes his "X," and his effort to argue whether that "X" is good or bad defines his essay as an evaluation argument.

To appreciate the organization of his argument, students need only consult p. 294 in the text, where a structure is suggested that describes Isaacson's essay to a tee. Thus, he begins in the opening two paragraphs by introducing his issue (using an anecdote taken from personal experience to explain what inspired his thinking about it) and then goes on to explain just what he thinks makes it so controversial, not as an issue dividing heterosexuals and homosexuals in the way that the issue is so often represented, but rather as an issue dividing members of the gay community itself. After announcing his alignment with those he characterizes as the "integrationists" who favor gay marriage, he proceeds in paragraphs 4 and 5 to summarize the views of those in the gay community who are opposed to legalizing gay marriage, a group he identifies as the "liberationists." Significantly, his summary appears unbiased and undistorted, which helps him to generate ethical appeal. In paragraph 5, Isaacson respectfully acknowledges his agreement with many of the arguments of the opposing view, thereby conceding their legitimacy. Nevertheless, however much he may sympathize with the opposing view, he remains ultimately convinced of the legitimacy of his claim and so concludes the paragraph by presenting it: "legalizing gay marriage would bring valuable benefits to gays and society as a whole."

The rest of the essay he devotes to supporting that claim, with reasons that his transitions enable readers to easily identify. Paragraph 6 ("First of all") conveys reason 1: legalizing gay marriage would enable gays to benefit from the "stabilizing force of marriage." In the course of substantiating that reason, he refutes the liberationists' criticism of marriage as an institution that imposes a limitation on personal freedom by implicitly arguing that marriage encourages a greater good; we must be willing, Isaacson implies, to sacrifice personal freedom for the greater good of the well-being of society. Significantly, he also expends some effort in arguing the warrant (i.e., a notion something along the lines that an institution that exercises a stablizing influence in our lives is a good one). Thus, the virtues of a "stablizing force" are made more concrete in the observations about children needing a stable environment and people in general tending to be happier in stable, long-term relationships. Paragraph 7 ("Second") conveys a second reason for or benefit to legalizing gay marriage: because doing so would convey on gays the "numerous legal rights of marriage that the straight comunity enjoys." If there is a weakness here, it may lie in the writer's failure to develop and support to a greater degree the warrant for this point (i.e., the notion that the numerous legal rights enjoyed by the straight, married community are worth having); as other participants in this conversation have pointed out, the consequences of being denied many of these rights, as gays presently are in most places, are considerable. Paragraph 8 ("Further") contains yet another reason in support of the writer's claim in maintaining gays would benefit in still another way from being able to legally marry in that marriage would confer upon their relationships a respectability and recognition that "gay love is just as meaningful as straight love." Paragraph 9, beginning appropriately with "Finally," introduces the last argument offered by the writer in support of his claim, the notion that legalizing gay marriage would enable gays to confront conservatives who conceive of marriage solely as the union of a man and a women and work to change their conception from within, as full-fledged members of society rather than as members of a marginalized group.

All in all, students are apt to find Isaacson's essay persuasive. Of course, to encourage them to learn from his example, instructors should take steps to ensure that students understand and appreciate the reasons behind any favorable assessment of the essay's persuasive power. One method for doing so would be to ask students to construct "says" and "does" statements for each paragraph and for the essay as a whole, and to do so before they try to write an evaluation argument of their own.

- **Debra Goodwin, "Beauty Pageant Fallacies" (pp. 302-303)**
There is nothing particularly surprising in Debra Goodwin's evaluation of beauty pageants, but this freshman writer does a good job at inventing an argument and providing grounds for support. Anticipating objections that her sister Pam's experience may be unrepresentative (the "hasty generalization" fallacy), Goodwin brings in testimony from a retired beauty pageant organizer, who claims that "diseases such as anorexia and bulimia are very common problems in the beauty pageant ring." Teachers might point out Goodwin's effective use of interview evidence throughout paragraph 2. Similarly, her use of analogy in paragraph 3 (comparing beauty pageants to dog or livestock shows) and of a clarifying example in paragraph 4 (Vanessa Williams) shows effective use of other kinds of grounds. Her quoted testimony in paragraph 2 also creates an effective <u>pathetic</u> appeal in its depersonalizing portrayal of the beauty queen who needs to work on her legs and get a better bra. Women students reading this essay point admirably to the penultimate paragraph, where Goodwin argues that beauty pageants stereotype woman's sexuality. By having to be sexy, yet wholesome, beauty queens project the image of women as eternal tease--scantily dressed but never nude.

Supporters of beauty pageants can proffer a defense. Why single out beauty pageants, they might say, when the whole of society--advertisements, fashion magazines, movies and television, the diet industry, and so forth--reinforces the image of the slim, youthful beauty? Beauty pageants don't cause our admiration for beauty, but merely reflect it. Women buy the beauty products and the fashion magazines, and women voluntarily choose to compete in beauty pageants. Besides, beauty pageants provide wonderful economic opportunities for women in the form of scholarships, endorsements, and careers in fashion or entertainment. Also, they will say, beauty pageants value the contestant's personality in their criteria for talent and for extemporaneous speaking. But these counter-arguments, to us at least, pale in the face of Debra Goodwin's well-argued condemnation.

ESSAYS FROM CHAPTER 14 (PROPOSAL)

• Jeffrey Cain, "A Proposal to Save Bernie's Blintzes Restaurant" (pp. 323-329)

This student essay is an example of a practical proposal, the kind that many students will have occasion to write during their careers. For that reason, proposal writing assignments often assume a reality for and a commitment from students that no other kind of writing assignment ever does; provided they take the assignment seriously, the result is often arguments that demonstrate a clearer conception of and a more sensitive response to the demands of a particular rhetorical situation than the writers have been able to accomplish before. Unfortunately, students often find other persons' practical proposals uninteresting because they are rooted in a personal, non-sharable content. This one may be no exception. Still, if students can be led to suspend their usual preference for a shared problem or issue, they can discover that this argument is well conceived, well presented, and well argued.

Before turning to the proposal proper, instructors should take special care to call students' attention to the letter of transmittal. More than a mere formality, this letter, they should notice, goes a great distance toward preparing the intended audience to be receptive to the writer's argument. It might be noted, for example, how the letter conveys the writer's professional attitude from the outset, thereby implicitly arguing one of his qualifications for submitting a proposal in the first place. From the very appearance of this letter, the intended auditor is immediately encouraged to believe that this proposal is no mere half-baked idea the writer is casually suggesting; compare the impression the writer would have conveyed had he simply dashed off a handwritten note on looseleaf notebook paper. This letter also provides the writer with a more graceful occasion than a formal essay might to spell out the qualifications he possesses that would incline an audience to believe that his proposal is worth listening to; thus, he is careful to identify himself as someone who knows this particular business from the inside out, as an employee, as someone familiar with the restaurant's economic troubles, and as someone who shares the owner's interest in it and in the culture it represents. Then, too, the letter enables the writer to introduce the nature of his proposal and so provoke the reader's interest by representing it as a relatively inexpensive alternative to the $60,000 plan proposed by the restaurant consultant. All in all, the letter enables the writer to accomplish a great deal of work in a brief space. Provided that it is well written, it works to enable writers to get a foot in the door.

Just as with the letter of transmittal, matters of form continue to play a role in the proposal itself in persuading the audience, and so students should be encouraged to spend some time appreciating how the various features (such as the division of the text into the various parts, the headings and sub-headings given to these parts, the typeface, and the layout) function.

Of even greater importance, however, is the nature of the writer's proposal argument itself. In an effort to appreciate the strengths of Cain's proposal, students may begin by noting how the text moves from a description of the problem to a description of the proposed solution to a justification for that solution, and in doing so, conforms in its overall structure to the three parts recommended for a proposal argument in this chapter. Students might then be prompted to consider what each of these three parts contributes to Cain's overall argument. In this context, they should not overlook the way in which Cain's careful description of the problem works to promote ethical appeal. Clearly, the intended audience does not need this rehearsal of the problem that includes a detailed account of the history of the business; anyone who has hired a professional consultant to solve the problem is probably well acquainted with what that problem is--or at least may be less likely to look to an amateur for a better explanation. What that audience seeks from the writer's explanation of the problem is not so much a better understanding of that problem but the assurance that the writer about to propose a solution is sufficiently knowledgeable about the problem to lend any solution he might offer some credibility. In short, what Cain has to demonstrate in describing the problem is that he knows what that problem is and that he is thus qualified to propose a way to solve it. Students should be able to locate the various strategies he resorts to in this section that enable him to do so, including his analysis of the problems of the consultant's proposal.

As for Cain's presentation of his proposal itself, it should be noted how he avoids some of the problems students typically encounter here, such as a failure to describe the proposal in sufficient detail to convince an audience that they have actually worked out all the details of its implementation. What they often forget is that this section is or should be inherently an argument, designed not merely to explain the proposal but to convince an audience that it is workable. For this purpose, mere assurances on the part of the writer are not enough. Hence, Cain here demonstrates through the degree of specificity of his argument that he has actually imagined how his proposal would be implemented and has done the research to acquire the necessary facts to convince someone else. Note, for example, the degree of specificity in paragraph 14, where Cain works out the costs of the cookies, and in paragraph 15, where he discusses possibilities for their distribution.

Finally, there is the justification section, where Cain argues explicitly why his proposal should be adopted, basing his reasons primarily upon arguments of consequence (although the first could also be interpreted as derived from an argument of precedent). These reasons are carefully enumerated and distinguished from the others for the convenience of the audience, making it easy for students to identify and to evaluate them. Again, it should be stressed that mere assertions of likely consequences are inadequate to the task here. Accordingly, students should be urged to take notice of the various ways in which Cain goes to some lengths to establish the legitimacy of the consequences he claims for his proposal. Nevertheless, in evaluating his reasons and the refutation he offers to would-be skeptics tempted to criticize his plan as too naive and simplistic, students will ultimately want to imagine ways Cain might have made his argument even stronger.

• Stephen Bean, "What Should Be Done About the Mentally Ill Homeless?" (pp. 330-338)

Bean's argument speaks directly to Krauthammer's (and others included in the Anthology section), shifting the focus from the mental health issue per se to a number of related social and economic issues. Bean describes four of Krauthammer's assumptions as flawed: that the homeless were spawned by deinstitutionalization of mental hospitals in the 60s; that the mentally ill comprise a large percentage of the homeless population; that the causes of homelessness among the mentally ill are psychological more than socio-economic; that institutionalization in asylums is the proper way to treat mentally ill homeless people.

Bean's arguments against the second two assumptions are both more significant and more persuasive than his arguments against the first two assumptions. On the question of numbers, Bean's evidence would not seem to gainsay definitively Krauthammer's minimal estimate of 25%. (Bean later presents a much lower estimate--5 to 7%--of those needing acute inpatient care of the sort called for by Krauthammer.) However, in raising the question of numbers, Bean points to the problem of using statistics in argumentation. How does one determine what percentage of the homeless are mentally ill? How does one tell whether mental illness caused homelessness or whether living on the streets caused symptoms of mental illness? What are we to do when the experts disagree--in this case radically?

As to the question of whether or not deinstitutionalization played a major role in the current homelessness phenomenon, it seems important first as a means of helping to estimate the numbers of homeless mentally ill. But it is important secondly because it is the anchoring link in Krauthammer's causal chain: If today's problem of homelessness was primarily caused by the emptying out of the nation's mental institutions, then reopening those institutions ought to go a long way toward solving the problem. Bean hopes to show that homelessness resulted primarily from loss of low-end jobs and elimination of single-room occupancy housing. He thus attempts to counter Krauthammer's causal assumption that deinstitutionalization played a major role in today's homelessness problem.

On the question of the current underlying (as opposed to historical) causes of homelessness, Bean seems to be on solid ground. He presents powerful evidence that lack of resources rather than lack of sanity constitutes the critical problem for homeless people. In turn, his suggestion that community-based care is less expensive and at least as effective as institutionalization is difficult to refute. And his conclusion, that the appeal of Krauthammer's argument lies in the fact that it places the homeless in a category separate from us, thereby licensing us to move them out of sight, is insightful.

ESSAYS FROM CHAPTER 15 (ETHICAL ARGUMENTS)

- **Ursula Le Guin, "The Ones Who Walk Away from Omelas" (pp. 349-353)**

In the context of this chapter, Le Guin's essay is useful for several reasons. First of all, it sets out the conflict between consequentialist arguments and arguments based on principles in the clearest possible terms. On the other hand, it also shows the power of language to give presence to a position that is pragmatically weak. Finally, it raises complex questions about the ethical responsibility of the individual within a society intolerant of individual differences.

In apparently "loading the dice" for the consequentialist position, Le Guin is tacitly undercutting that position. She does this in two ways. First, she creates a society that is ideal to the point of being unlivable, a utopia that raises in our minds the whole question of "What would I live for if all my dreams came true?" Secondly, in the process of persuading her audience that they really could live here and enjoy it, she calls our attention to the arbitrary and fabricated nature of the place. If "we" don't like something, she will always change it to suit our sense of what utopia should be.

So, our consequentialist utopia is more likely to make us nervous than it is to make us truly happy. Her tour of Omelas will cause some to question their whole utilitarian outlook on things (and our experience suggests that students are generally utilitarian in outlook and find questioning some of these assumptions a useful exercise).

Meanwhile, the unreality of Omelas is in stark contrast to the very concrete reality of the suffering child who supposedly underwrites the dream by its suffering. The "presence" of the child, the simple particulars of her description of its suffering, make it realer than the whole universe she's just finished recommending to us. And, to frame the question in terms of the phrase Le Guin borrows from William James, is the child's destructive suffering truly necessary to the happiness of the denizens of Omelas? Until the point we encounter the child, everything is negotiable, fabricated, all part of a human construct. But suddenly, the necessity of the child's suffering is an absolute, unquestionable assumption. Why? The principle affirmed by those who leave Omelas is precisely that the necessity is false, a dream from which they have awakened and to which they can't return (though many of your students will want them to "stay and fight").

ESSAYS FROM CHAPTER 17 (USING AND DOCUMENTING SOURCES)

- **Michael Levin, "The Case for Torture" (pp. 387-389)**

Levin's argument is an interesting mirror of Le Guin's. Instead of a single individual suffering in order that large numbers of people can enjoy the good life, Levin's scenario considers the possibility that the single individual's suffering can prevent the destruction of large numbers of people. As Le Guin's scenario loads the dice in favor of a non-utilitarian principle, Levin's loads them in favor of a consequentialist conclusion. It's much easier to see the ends justifying the means in Levin's case than it is in Le Guin's: Levin's suffering individual is not innocent, he's a moral monster whose suffering will save many innocent lives.

Levin gains an important concession from his audience by his opening example which pits the destruction of Manhattan against a couple of hours of torture for an odious individual. To stand on principle in this case seems absurd. Worse, it seems an act of "moral cowardice," keeping our own hands clean at the expense of millions of people. What Levin is using here, and uses throughout his essay, are the sorts of extreme case examples that philosophers are fond of in probing principles and axioms for exceptions. What is given in each case is that the identity of the terrorist is known without a doubt, that torture will surely produce confession, that confession will allow us to thwart the terrorist, and that what the terrorist was up to involved the destruction of many innocent lives.

Levin labels "disingenuous" those who would contrast the certitude of his scenarios to the murkier complexities of real life. And yet it seems crucial to ask how sure we need to be before torture is legitimated. By way of contrast, consider a situation in which the authorities know that one of two people put a bomb on a plane, but didn't know which one. Would it be legitimate to torture both, including one we know must be innocent, in order to save those lives? And consider too the ambiguities inherent in the concept terrorist. The Shah of Iran, for example, regularly used torture both as a punishment (which Levin is careful to exclude from his argument) and as a means of "preventing future evils." In many cases, the people tortured were certainly "terrorists" bent on disrupting the civil order of Iran. But over the long term, the policy of torture weakened respect for government, set up a relationship of mistrust between a government and its people, contributed to a cycle of vengeance that created yet another wave of "terrorists" bent on avenging the suffering of their predecessors.

In sum, Levin's argument is feasible only if we accept the certitude of all the conditions of his scenarios. Many of us may give assent to the use of torture in all his scenarios, and yet balk at the principle that a person who has acted in an uncivilized manner "can have no complaint if civilization tries to thwart him by whatever means necessary." Many of us may well wish to leave Levin's scenarios as exceptions to the rule that when a society forgoes its civility it ceases to be a civilized society.

V. ANALYSIS OF READINGS IN PART FIVE: AN ANTHOLOGY OF ESSAYS

In this section of the Instructor's Manual, we continue to provide close analyses of readings, albeit this time, of readings provided in the Anthology that concludes our text. Our intention here, as in the previous section, is to help instructors regard the readings not necessarily as "models for students to emulate" but as "contributions to a conversation," full of strengths and weaknesses. To help students understand and appreciate the strengths and weaknesses of these arguments, instructors might adopt the suggestion provided in the For Class Discussion exercise that concludes each topic unit and encourage students to analyze and discuss the readings using the "Guide Questions for the Analysis and Evaluation of Arguments" that prefaces the anthology (pp. 455-456); or students might be encouraged to apply the appropriate supplemental checklist provided for each of the various kinds of arguments in Section III of this Instructor's Manual, or the Toulmin scheme charted on p. 103 of the text, or some combination of analytical tools. Our commentary below may help initiate a productive class discussion of the readings as well.

As a preliminary to any such discussion, however, instructors may also want to urge their students to consult the Acknowledgments section that concludes the text in an effort, consistent with strategies outlined in Chapter 2 for improving their reading process, to have them locate and recover some of the original context for the articles they have been assigned to read in terms of the nature of the original source of the articles and the dates they were published. No doubt some students, especially more novice readers and writers, would even benefit from a demonstration in class of how to interpret and what to infer about an article from a particular citation.

Finally, it may be worth pointing out that students seem to read better, more closely and more thoughtfully, when they are asked to produce something in writing based on their reading that prepares for or that lends some closure to a class discussion. For that purpose, having students write out responses to whatever analysis questions the instructor prescribes works perfectly well. Another interesting alternative that gives students an opportunity to practice adopting a perspective not necessarily their own on a given issue is to ask them to analyze one writer's argument from the point of view of another writer on that same topic--to consider, for example, how Mike Romano, author of "In Defense of Decency," might critique the argument presented by Marc Rothenberg in "The Net Doesn't Need Thought Police."

IMMIGRATION POLICY

- **Julian Simon, "The Case for Greatly Increased Immigration"**
- **Michael Lind, "Huddled Excesses"**
- **Dan Stein, "Timeout: The United States Needs a Moratorium on Immigration"**

Like those on the topic "Legalization of Drugs," these arguments afford instructors plenty of opportunity to alert students to the difficulties posed by the use of statistics, for all three rely to varying degrees in making their cases on various numbers and computations that each appears capable of manipulating for his own purposes. Encouraging students to develop a healthy skepticism when confronted by such evidence is probably not a bad idea, particularly given most novice readers' inclination to put their faith in such "facts." As a result, students might find it helpful to contextualize these readings with a study of Chapter 6, "Evidence in Argument."

It ought not be lost on students how the title of Julian Simon's article announces the writer's subject and purpose--to address the issue-question "Should we permit substantially increased immigration in the U.S.?" to which Simon responds with an argument supporting the claim, "Yes, we should permit substantially increased immigration because a substantial increase in the number of immigrants ultimately benefits the citizens of the U.S." Thus does this article identify itself as primarily a causal argument, although Simon concludes by offering several proposals for strengthening our immigration policy apart from merely admitting more immigrants.

Given that one of the warrants behind Simon's claim is the assumption that present immigration rates are by no means substantial enough to realize those benefits, he begins arguing his case proper by refuting those who believe that immigration rates are already at a record level. To this end, he explains the need to appreciate the difference between absolute numbers of immigrants and their proportion to the native population, which in turn prompts him to conclude that "We are a nation not of immigrants, but rather the descendants of immigrants."

Having argued that, contrary to popular belief, present immigration rates are relatively low, Simon proceeds to point out the benefits of greatly increasing those rates, refuting as he does so those who maintain that the costs of such an increase would be overwhelming. Thus, in response to those who claim that increased immigration would deplete capital resources, Simon acknowledges that immigration does indeed create a need for more hospitals and schools, but argues that the immigrants themselves pay a substantial share through their taxes, and in fact, "pay much more in taxes than they receive in benefits." In response to those who claim that immigrants take away jobs from native workers and so foster increasing native unemployment, Simon argues that the research simply doesn't support such a claim, indicating instead that immigrants tend to create jobs either through their purchases or their own industry in opening new businesses.

Finally, having argued what he believes to be the considerable benefits that increased immigration offers the U.S. and its citizens, Simon is moved to examine and to respond to what he calls the "real reasons" behind the (irrational) opposition to increased immigration, reasons that he locates ultimately in a nativism or racism that he suggests has its roots in the earliest days of our country. He then concludes his essay with various proposals for improving our immigration policies, apart from increasing the rate of immigration, to maximize the benefits he insists will occur.

Overall, Simon's article represents a classical argument, one most students should have little difficulty understanding, provided they attend to the various cues Simon provides. In fact, it may well be worthwhile before leaving the essay to prompt students to locate and attend to the various strategies Simon employs to ensure that his rather lengthy argument is relatively easy to follow. In this context, you'll want to be sure to call their attention to his introduction, particularly to the way it prepares for the argument to follow in spelling out Simon's claim and summarizing his case to the point of enumerating the various benefits that he will later discuss and the arguments of the opposition that he plans to refute.

One word of caution here: for the most part, Simon organizes the body of his essay according to the views of those opposed to immigration; thus, his strategy is to present a claim advanced by those opposed to immigration and then to refute that claim with evidence consisting largely of statistics. In short, this strategy could be represented as follows: "Some people claim X, but, in fact, X is not true/is wrong/is not supported by the evidence." (See, for example, paragraph 15 vs. paragraphs 16 and 17, or paragraph 18 vs. paragraph 19, or paragraph 23 vs. paragraphs 24ff.) Unfortunately, novice readers occasionally have trouble recognizing this strategy for what it is and become confused, interpreting such strategies as evidence that the writer is somehow contradicting himself, saying two things at once. For them, it might be useful to point out Simon's use of this strategy, calling their attention to the transitions that mark his movement from a rehearsal of an opposing view to his own refutation.

No doubt Simon's status and expertise as a "noted economist" lends his statistics a credibility that they might otherwise not have; nevertheless, as readers, we may well be moved to wonder what all of his statistics have to say about the individual person and the various ways in which his or her life might be affected by immigration. It is one thing to claim that, if native workers are displaced by an influx of immigrants, such displacement "is too little to be observable"; it is quite another to be or to know the worker who has actually been displaced. When we start asking questions about just which U.S. citizens stand to gain economically from increased immigration and which may ultimately suffer, we enter the domain of Michael Lind's article. Like Simon's piece, Lind's also represents a what is essentially causal argument, albeit one diametrically opposed in its main claim to Simon's. (At the same time, in his effort to anticipate an opposing view and so characterize the reduction in immigration as a liberal cause that "has nothing to do with the absurd and offensive claims of some conservatives," Lind also makes use of the strategies of definition arguments as described in Chapter 10.)

Contrary to Simon, Lind argues a resounding "No!" in response to the issue-question "Should we permit substantially increased immigration in the U.S.?" contending that while increased immigration may well be great for "business," it actually hurts poor Americans as well as those of the working and middle classes. Although offering considerably less evidence in support of his claim than did Simon, Lind counters the "facts" Simon presents with some statistics and examples of his own in his effort to show that immigrants deprive native citizens of the opportunity to be trained for high-tech jobs and are far more likely to receive welfare benefits. Students will surely recognize the extent to which Lind's assertions appear to directly contradict certain claims made by Simon (e.g., compare Lind's claims above with these from Simon: "U.S. immigrants pay much more in taxes than they receive in benefits" [paragraph 19] and "a good-sized body of competent recent research shows that immigration does not exacerbate unemployment" [paragraph 25].) A productive discussion might prompt students to consider which of the two arguments seems the more persuasive and why. It might be suggested that Lind's argument for limiting immigration is ultimately somewhat hampered by the writer's effort to address what are really two issues at once--not only the issue of whether immigration should be limited but also the issue of whether arguing for such limits is a conservative or liberal cause.

Stein's article recalls both the argument by Simon and the argument by Lind. Like Lind, Stein also argues for setting limits on immigration--in fact, he seeks a complete moratorium on immigration to enable us to assimilate those immigrants who are already here, to revise our legal immigration policies, and to devise better policies for stopping illegal immigration. (Be sure, by the way, that students understand what a "moratorium" is, for Stein never really defines it in the course of his article.) At the same time, in his proposal that we limit the immigration of extended families and promote instead the immigration of those capable of making "a positive contribution to this country," he appears to support Simon's notion of the need for a merit-based system for selecting new immigrants.

In any event, Stein starts right out with "a few facts to set the record straight," and so begins with a bit of definitional sleight of hand. In opposing immigration, Stein assures his readers, he is not going against "tradition"; rather he is recuperating a lost tradition of balanced immigration, where peaks of high immigration are followed by valleys of low immigration. Stein's identification with tradition is in keeping with every proposer's concern not to appear too radical.

In support of his claim that we need a "respite" from untraditionally high levels of immigration, Stein offers the following reasons: 1. it would afford us time to absorb immigrants into the American mainstream; 2. it would afford us time to develop more realistic immigration policies; 3. it would afford us time to figure out how to deal with the huge backlog of immigrant applications; 4. it would free up manpower to deal with the problem of illegal immigration, which in turn contributes to terrorism in this country.

Beyond his citation of the Trade Center bombing, and his assertion that immigration is severely stretching local public services, Stein offers little concrete evidence in these reasons for the negative consequences of immigration. (Certainly, many would take issue with Stein's assumption that the reluctance of immigrants to join the American melting pot is bad.) Stein's reasons simply come down to a matter of buying time to forge solutions to a problem that he has spent little time proving to be serious.

Stein is more persuasive that his proposal could be enacted. His idea of having social security cards function like ATM cards and of shifting the onus for enforcement from employers to the government has face validity. His argument for the redefinition of "family" to exclude extended family, meanwhile, is problematic in the same way that his assumption that immigrants should "melt" into the pot is problematic. The norm of the nuclear family is, after all, a cultural norm not universally shared.

MERCY KILLING AND THE RIGHT TO DIE

- James Rachels, "Active and Passive Euthanasia"
- David B. McCurdy, "Saying What We Mean"
- William May, "Rising to the Occasion of Our Death"

Rachels' argument exploits strategies characteristic of several different kinds of arguments, including ethical arguments, definition arguments, and, to some degree, arguments of consequence, and does so with considerably skill. Writing expressly to urge doctors to reconsider their support for the traditional distinction endorsed by the AMA between active and passive euthanasia (paragraph 1), Rachel argues the claim that doctors should not accept the doctrine that "it is permissible . . . to withhold treatment and allow a patient to die, but it is never permissible to take any direct action designed to kill the patient" (p. 473). The reasons he offers in support of this claim are three: 1) because active euthanasia can on occasion be more consistent with humanitarian impulses to end suffering than passive euthanasia is (paragraphs 2-4); 2) because the distinction between active and passive euthanasia "leads to decisions concerning life and death made on irrelevant grounds" (paragraphs 5-8); and 3) because there is finally no moral difference between active euthanasia (i.e.,killing) and passive euthanasia (i.e., letting die) [paragraphs 9-14]. For evidence, he relies not upon facts and statistics--given that he is arguing essentially a moral or ethical issue, it would be difficult to imagine how he could use such support to any great degree--but rather strives to make a convincing case by resorting to concrete (albeit hypothetical) examples, analogies, and additional reasoning that demonstrates, for example, the logical inconsistencies in opposing points of view. (Indeed, instructors might ask students whether it would have strengthened Rachels' case had he supported his claim that, say, active euthanasia is no less moral than passive euthanasia by citing statistics that indicated that 65% of the population agreed with him.) Rachels appears to anticipate that his audience would not object to the warrants behind the reasons supporting his claim (e.g., the warrant behind reason no. 2: decisions about life and death made on irrelevant grounds are to be avoided) and thus does not devote much discussion to providing backing for them. (Nevertheless, the article by May will take issue with at least one of Rachels' warrants [the one that underlies his notion that active euthanasia can be preferable to passive euthanasia as a more effective means to end suffering] by denying that an action taken to end suffering is necessarily good--see the discussion of May's argument below).

Overall, Rachels makes a persuasive case in support of his claim. Given the nature of that claim, his examples and analogies are pretty convincing, having been contrived to represent situations even a lay audience should have no difficulty accepting as situations that doctors confront daily in the so-called "real world." His ethical appeal is likewise solid, as it must be to enable him to sidestep any suspicion that he argues his case out of anything other than the very highest motives. The situations he contrives reveal him to be a compassionate person and one sensitive to the concerns of those espousing opposing views (a man of good will), one fully aware of and knowledgeable about the various ramifications of his position (a man of good sense), and one who seems to be most interested in promoting what can he thinks can ultimately be shown to be The Good (a man of good moral character). Where his argument weakens, one could argue, is in its concluding paragraph, where he suddenly seems to back away from promoting the next logical step in this argument, leaving a reader somewhat confused as to his ultimate intention. Understandably, he does not want to conclude by arguing that, since there is no moral difference between active and passive euthanasia, his audience should now resolve to break the law by performing active euthanasia; yet, it is difficult to believe that he has gone to the lengths he has in his article simply to convince doctors that "they should not give the distinction any added authority and weight by writing it into official statements." Perhaps a more fitting conclusion, that is, one the article itself seems to be preparing for, might have been to urge doctors to (at least) consider working toward changing that law to take into account the argument that Rachels advances.

Unlike Rachels, McCurdy seems unaware of (or, at least, unconcerned about) any need to make a formal distinction between active and passive euthanasia, defining euthanasia in his opening paragraph simply as "an action or an omission of treatment motivated by mercy" (p. 477). Yet, as that definition implies, his essay, like Rachels', exploits strategies of both definition arguments and arguments of consequence.

In this case, these strategies are put to use in defending the claim, expressed on p. 479, that "those who would deny life-sustaining treatments in order to conserve resources should not be allowed, let alone encouraged, to call the consequences of their proposal 'euthanasia'. People should be pressed to adopt a more truthful label." In other words, as the title of this essay implies, McCurdy is determined to take people to task for misusing the term "euthanasia" in ways that appear to equate euthanasia with an effort to save money. His reasons for taking the stance that he does are a bit difficult to discern in spots but appear to be these: 1) because those who identify euthanasia with an efforts to save money distort sincere arguments in favor of euthanasia as an effort to exercise compassion in relieving suffering; 2) because any identification of euthanasia with a drive to save money undercuts the possibility of future, productive dialogue on the issue; and 3) because an association of euthanasia with crude utilitarianism ultimately obscures the moral challenge that euthanasia represents for the church.

Because McCurdy's argument is based upon an assumption that people are indeed misusing the term "euthanasia" in ways that associate it with economic concerns, the author spends a considerable part of his essay as he must documenting occurrences of the misuse of the term and so substantiating that warrant (see paragraphs 3-10). Nevertheless, one cannot help but question whether the relatively few examples he cites of what he perceives to be a misuse of the term are finally sufficient to convince an audience that such misuse of the term signals the alarming trend that McCurdy seems to think it does.

Would that McCurdy had devoted as much space as he does trying to establish the existence of a trend of misuse to explaining and substantiating his supporting reasons. What actual evidence does he present that the misuse of the term will have or has had the consequences he claims? To help an audience understand the seriousness of his concerns and the extent of the problem, McCurdy needs to do more than simply <u>assert</u> possible consequences.

And finally, just what would McCurdy have his audience <u>do</u>? How would he have them respond to his argument? He says that those who misuse the term "euthanasia" "should not be allowed" to do so, that they should be "pressed to adopt a more truthful label," but just how does he imagine his audience doing so? What action can or should they take? Without some concrete guidance, that audience is left floundering, ultimately not only not quite sure of the nature of McCurdy's complaint, but also not quite convinced about how seriously they should take it.

Unlike McCurdy's essay, May's represents a direct response to Rachels' in the form of an argument that challenges one of Rachels' key warrants, the assumption that the relief of another's suffering is necessarily good or desirable. Taking Rachels' argument to its logical conclusion, May identifies on p. 480 the issue his argument will address: "Should we develop a judicious, regulated social policy permitting voluntary euthanasia for the terminally ill?" May's answer is no, and the reasons he gives serve to remind us of the dangers of taking an audience's assent to our warrants for granted. Contrary to believing that the relief of suffering is necessarily a good thing, May actually suggests the opposite, contending that the act of suffering represents an opportunity for us to "rise to the occasion of our death." His notion here seems to be that the act of suffering can represent a good for the sufferer him- or herself, for "the best death is not always the sudden death." Not surprisingly, no doubt in part out of a fear of damaging his ethical appeal, May does not pursue this line of argument. Rather he moves on to offer several other reasons that we ought not engage in mercy killing: for one, he claims, it would deprive the dying (and perhaps their loved ones--May is not crystal clear on this point in his reference to "those forewarned of death and given time to prepare for it") of the opportunity to "engage in acts of reconciliation" (again, an unclear phrase--by "acts of reconciliation" does he mean the act of reconciling oneself to one's impending death or the act of reconciling with the dying or with others from whom one has been estranged?). It is difficult not to interpret May's vagueness on these points as the product of a deliberate effort to avoid giving offense to his audience.

Other reasons for allowing patients, in May's words, to "do their own dying," include the opportunity such a policy provides for relatives to be forewarned of the patient's death, thereby enabling them to experience "advanced grieving" which, May contends "may ease some of their pain." Just as important, yet another reason May offers in support of his claim is the notion that the community ultimately benefits from exposure to the virtues that the dying "sometimes evince"; to kill dying patients off quickly would deprive that community of much needed models.

Needless to say, May's reasons for arguing the position that he does are sure to provoke discussion among students, no matter how much some may be inclined to sympathize with his assertion that "hard cases do not always make good laws or wise social policies." Undoubtedly his argument is considerably weak in spots. Despite an effective refutation of the argument that active euthanasia represents a patient's opportunity to determine his or her own destiny, May's logical appeal suffers, for example, from his apparent failure to acknowledge that an act of active euthanasia need not necessarily eliminate opportunities for reconciliation (of whatever sort), for advanced grieving, or for community education and growth from the example of the dying. The very causes that May advances for taking the position he does, in other words, are not necessary to obtaining his desired effects. Nor does his argument gain much from any effort to generate ethical appeal. While his willingness to acknowledge the rare circumstance in which mercy killing would be justified (in Toulmin language, the "qualifier" he provides in paragraph 8) goes some distance toward demonstrating that he is a reasonable person of good will, one cannot help but regard him as somewhat cold and unfeeling when he argues that dying patients should not have the right to be killed because their suffering can be a positive experience for them and for their community. One might well be moved to question whether his position would change were he to find himself or one of his loved ones suffering unbearably and unremittingly from some fatal illness. All in all, what he appears to need here is a stronger pathetic appeal; ironically, his best effort at engaging the imaginative sympathies of his audience comes in paragraph 8, when he describes a situation calling for some qualification of his position.

It would be an interesting exercise to have students imagine how Rachels and May would debate one another on this issue; the assignment designated as Option 4 on p. 76 would provide a formal opportunity for them to do so.

THE RESPONSIBILITY OF THE RICH FOR THE POOR

- Garrett Hardin, "Lifeboat Ethics: The Case Against Helping the Poor"

- Peter Singer, "Rich and Poor"

Peter Singer's argument offers a wealth of illustrative material for anyone trying to model good arguments. He defines key terms ("absolute poverty" and "absolute affluence") at the outset of his argument; he uses statistics forcefully to lend presence to his arguments (note for example how he contrasts the .39 percent of GNP that Britain expends on development assistance to the 5.5 percent it expends on alcohol); he carefully considers the opposing arguments without converting them to straw; he lays out the premises of his argument in syllogistic form so that we can readily see his assumptions and the implications of those assumptions; he follows good "Nestorian order" by dealing with the strongest argument (the ethics of triage) last; and he consciously addresses concerns from both the consequentialist and non-consequentialist points of view.

Having established the seriousness and depth of the problem with his grim drum roll of statistics, and having established the nature of the problem as one of distribution not production or "transfer" (the absolutely affluent can certainly transfer a great deal to the absolutely poor without sacrificing anything of "comparable moral significance") Singer is in a position to meet the objections to his argument. He considers four objections. The first three basically address various egoistic positions that deny the obligation to assist on the grounds that the welfare of the person being beseeched comes before the welfare of those doing the beseeching. For example, to those who say "I have negative rights not to be interfered with--to say and do what I wish, to walk across campus, say, without being impeded." Singer in effect replies: "Yes, but I can also be inconvenienced if I meet another with a positive right to be assisted--a drowning child, say, encountered on my walk across campus."

Positive rights, in Singer's view, enjoy a privileged position vis-a-vis negative rights. Hence his belief that other people's positive rights, even if those people are separated by geography, race or class, take precedence over the negative rights of those close to me. And my property rights, perhaps the most obvious instance of negative rights, must yield to the positive rights of the poor. Whereas property rights, in that they comprise the foundation of capitalism, are for Carnegie sacred, they are for Singer a secondary consideration. Here, Singer cites Aquinas, who argues that what we possess in "superabundance is owed, of natural right, to the poor."

In refuting the first three opposing views, which stress selfishness, Singer emphasizes that chance rather than destiny contributes much to one person's being in the position to help another. Because all three views are essentially "pre-ethical," Singer's arguments would seem decisive.

With the fourth opposing view, however, Singer is faced with an ethical question which is in itself quite powerful--what if the long-term consequences of helping the poor are to increase their numbers and to worsen their dilemma? Singer counters by saying that in balancing outcomes, one must take probability as well as severity of outcome into account. He grants that if offering aid to poor countries now produces global catastrophe later, it doesn't make much sense. But how likely is it that giving aid will in fact produce global catastrophe? Here, contra Hardin, he produces an alternative scenario whereby giving aid might eventually lower the birth rate of the recipient countries and thereby bring long term as well as short term benefits. Now the argument hinges on which of the two scenarios seems more likely as opposed to which of the two positions is more moral (or even more pragmatic).

In his conclusion, Singer asks how we might determine what is of "comparable moral significance"? How do we determine what the absolutely affluent might transfer to the absolutely poor and have the moral books balance? Here Singer runs up against the problem of how people normally keep score in such cases. That is, most members of an absolutely affluent society like ours make that determination mostly on the basis of what others of their ilk normally do, not what anyone should ideally do. Few give until it hurts; most give until they've given about what everyone else has. Singer's argument sweeps away most of the rationalizations people offer for their behavior, but the underlying social/psychological motivations remain unaddressed. Odious as the Andrew Carnegie-like notion of <u>noblesse oblige</u> might seem to us, it at least created a powerful, indeed quasi-religious sense of charitable obligation in rich people. Singer's <u>noblesse</u>, meanwhile, has no <u>oblige</u>; few contemporary rich people--or poor people for that matter--would recognize any "natural" obligation by the rich to support the poor or to be their trustees. Hence, whatever strengths his argument might evince, it's hard to say how much luck he'll have in a culture traditionally concerned far more with individuals' negative rights and material successes than the positive rights of the world's poor.

With Hardin's essay we return to a position which is in many ways more conservative than that of old-style industrial capitalism that endorses private charity. Played out to its logical conclusion, Hardin's essay would seem to militate against any public sharing of resources and appears to reject the whole notion of positive rights among the poor. His is an extremely hard nosed form of consequentialist ethic with overtones of essentialist doctrine. Hardin begins, appropriately enough, with a critique of the environmental metaphor of "spaceship" earth which suggests the necessity of sharing limited resources in order for all to survive. In that Hardin's own essay uses a powerful mix of metaphorical resemblance arguments and statistics, he clearly recognizes the powerful grip that figurative language can have on readers. For Hardin, the environmental metaphor falls apart because there is nothing comparable to a captain on spaceship earth to oversee the distribution of resources. The sorts of catastrophes that overtake the passengers on a leaderless spaceship are of the very sort that plague the passengers in the "lifeboat" analogy at the heart of his essay.

In developing his counter metaphor, Hardin stresses several important differences between spaceships and lifeboats. First of all, many people are not already on board the lifeboat; more than twice the number of people in the lifeboat are in the water, presumably thrashing about for their very lives. The lifeboat itself could hold more people, but not many, and some space is needed in order to maximize the safety of the passengers. If all the people in the water got on the boat, it would sink; if some were let in, we might sink, and we'd certainly increase the danger to ourselves. By admitting none, we insure our continued safety. (To those in the boat who feel guilty about not letting anyone on board, Hardin suggests they jump into the water and let a swimmer take their place.)

It is, without a doubt, an extremely powerful, if upsetting representation of the world's resource problem. While he later suggests that poor people (or at least the governments of poor countries) mostly deserve their plights, he doesn't suggest here that those in the boat are there by dint of industry or entrepreneurial skill. As he notes in his conclusion, we have to accept conditions as we find them and not worry about trying to remake history. Those in the boat have material goods and negative rights; those outside the boat have no legitimate claim against either, and the whole question of virtue is beside the point.

One might well begin critiquing the lifeboat metaphor by asking, as would Singer, just how likely the scenario it implies might be. If we don't let people in the boat, we can be sure that many of them are going to drown. How sure are we that letting them aboard will doom all of us or even inconvenience us greatly? Hardin offers a number of historical precedents suggesting that resource sharing programs often have undesirable and unforeseen effects. And he offers a number of statistical projections suggesting that foreign aid and immigration programs would lead to insupportable populations containing an enormous proportion of impoverished peoples who would expand exponentially until doomsday.

How reliable are the projections? As always, they are tricky. Since the essay is now more than twenty years old, you might ask students to examine the accuracy of his projections so far. In lieu of that, however, you might refer to the global warming debate and the critique of statistical models discussed there. Critics of those models point up the problem of projecting outcomes based on present conditions when the conditions themselves may well change in response to some of the predicted changes. Singer makes a similar point here when he suggests that countries who receive aid are no longer as poor as they were before they received aid and changes in economic condition typically beget other changes, particularly in birthrates, which tend to go down as developing countries reach certain socio-economic plateaus.

Another problem with the lifeboat metaphor has to do with its rigidity. It's an all-or-nothing scenario in which every person added is the potential back breaking straw. Not only is it a world without margin for error, it's a world of "fixities and definites," and false dilemmas. In the world outside the metaphor, pitching oneself off the lifeboat isn't the only way of supporting the swimmers. As Singer and Carnegie both make clear, we can each choose to give up some portion of our resources according to some calculus of charity of our own devising. And each of the world's governments can follow the same procedure. Most of them do share their resources, usually out of some mixture of charitable feeling and a pragmatic desire to build up trading partners and mollify potential third world revolutionaries. (Some of the swimmers, it should be recalled in the spirit of realpolitik, have torpedoes--ever large ones.)

Hardin's subsequent metaphor of the commons is both less exciting and more logically compelling than his lifeboat metaphor. Certainly it has gripped the imagination of conservative American economists who've used it relentlessly over the past decade to promote the privatization of public resources. He offers a number of historic anecdotes supporting his view that taking away the incentives of ownership entails a drop in the quality of stewardship. While not fatal to the notion of sharing resources, the analogy strongly suggests that we need to look for different ways of distributing resources so as to increase all participants' sense of ownership. Indeed, in this regard, Hardin's argument might as likely support a case for a stronger world government as it does a case for less intergovernmental sharing.

CIVIL DISOBEDIENCE

- Martin Luther King, Jr., "Letter From Birmingham Jail"
- Lewis Van Dusen, "Civil Disobedience: Destroyer of Democracy"
- Plato, from <u>The Crito</u>

    King's open letter to his fellow clergymen represents a classic instance of the epistolary argument. Note how skillfully King exploits the strengths of the epistolary mode at the same time that he quietly compensates for some of the special limitations of the genre.
    Perhaps the most important advantage of using this form of argument lies in the intimate relationship it creates between author and reader. Even though we constitute a "secondary audience" for King's address, we still have the sense of listening in on someone speaking out of a very deep personal anguish and concern. Much of the authority for King's argument lies in the undeniable sincerity of the author and his personal involvement in the issue at hand. The letter constitutes a form of "testimony" that would be difficult to achieve in a more formal essay.
    And because of the nature of King's address, we don't expect the same sorts of evidence and documentation that we might well demand of an author speaking to us less directly and personally. Indeed, a barrage of data and citations would render the whole epistle implausible--who writes a letter like a legal brief? When King refers to the "hard brutal facts" about the evils of Birmingham, he simply mentions several generalizations without documenting his sources--and we have no trouble accepting that practice in a letter. King's ethos (based on his willingness to suffer for his cause in his narrow cell, on his elevated diction and charitable treatment of his opposition, on his references to canonical religious and political figures, and on his references to his leadership role) and richly imagistic passages drawn from personal experience carry far more weight here than they might in a straight persuasive essay.
    If letters allow us to draw more freely on personal experience, they present some formidable difficulties as well. In particular, King must speak to two audiences simultaneously.

Even if he speaks past his fellow clergymen to us, he must sustain the illusion of speaking to his primary audience to keep us engaged. In this regard, note how King draws on spiritual examples and authorities (e.g., Christ and Aquinas) that his putative audience is bound to acknowledge, while at the same time he invokes historical authorities (e.g., Lincoln and Jefferson) that speak powerfully to his lay audience. By the same token, King employs a sort of "double-decker" argument strategy that allows him to address both his audiences. For example, early in his essay he responds to the clergy's concern that the civil rights movement is the result of "outside" intervention. At one level, he denies the charge, carefully detailing how he was invited in and simply lived up to a promise made long before to local leadership. But he then moves the refutation up a level and argues that it doesn't matter whether he's an outsider: "Like Paul, I must constantly respond to the Macedonian call for aid. . . . Injustice anywhere is a threat to injustice everywhere."

He follows a similar pattern later in arguing that he's not an "extremist" like Elijah Muhammad and then saying that being an extremist (like Jesus) in opposition to a corrupt status quo is OK. And, contra the white clergy, he denies that the police have acted with restraint, invoking images of "dogs sinking teeth into unarmed, nonviolent Negroes" and of police slapping and striking women and children. But he then goes on to argue that even if the police were acting with restraint, how can we applaud them for protecting a corrupt system? In each case he first refutes a definitional claim (I am an extremist; the police belong to the class of those who act with restraint) on its own grounds and then proceeds to make a "higher" appeal to an ethical judgment about the goodness of the class itself.

King's letter is a remarkable defense of "extreme" behavior and a most reasonable proposal for dramatic action. His even tone, his balanced rhetoric, his "bi-level" arguments and appeals to authority and the looseness of the epistolary form allow him reach a broad audience. By detailing the causes of the civil rights impasse in a colorful narrative, he makes nonviolent civil disobedience seem almost an inevitable outcome (with all sorts of respectable precursors) rather than an anomalous disruption. And instead of being the "cause" of racial tension in the South, civil rights activists are portrayed as those who "merely bring to the surface the hidden tension that is already alive."

King is simultaneously a commentator on and actor in the drama he relates. The epistolary form offers him the perfect means of expression for both roles in that drama. Moreover it can also offer students an opportunity to move back and forth freely between personal experience and formal argumentation. Hence we recommend strongly giving them an opportunity to experiment with the mode.

At the outset of his attack on civil disobedience, Lewis Van Dusen, Jr. makes a distinction between legitimate and illegitimate forms of civil disobedience. According to his definition, legitimate civil disobedience must not test the validity of the law in order to sustain an individual suit; it must be openly committed; it must be nonviolent and noninterfering in others' rights; and the person disobeying must accept the penalties of law freely. Antigone and Socrates, among others, are cited here for exemplary acts of civil disobedience.

Van Dusen explicitly rejects King as a legitimate civil disobedient on the grounds that subsequent court decisions upheld King's view that the state laws he violated were legally as well as morally wrong (hence, King tested the validity of the law). Although it might serve Van Dusen's argument (which is being made, it needs to be remembered, in the late sixties shortly after Watts, Detroit, and the Chicago Convention) to exclude the recently martyred King from his opposition, he can't do so because King challenged the whole system, not just a single law. And he did so in the name of a higher law that Van Dusen can't afford to acknowledge.

Even the briefest examination of the <u>Crito</u> passage should clarify the incompatibility of King's and Van Dusen's arguments. Plato's argument against civil disobedience leaves no room for any legitimate form of disobedience. The contract between the state and individual requires unquestioning fealty from the individual who cannot disobey the state in any way without simultaneously threatening all civil institutions, betraying the good that the individual has enjoyed from the state, threatening the safety of his friends, and condemning himself to second-class citizenry and even banishment to Hades.

For Plato, the relationship between state and citizen, like the relationship between parent and child, is not a two-way street; the parent/state may punish, but the child/citizen may not strike back, nor may they question the justness of their punishment. (However powerful Plato's resemblance claim may have been in its day, our students don't typically find the appeal to an authoritarian family model particularly persuasive. Discussion of the issue here should help them understand the care one must take in developing analogies and the limits of resemblance arguments.)

In determining what's at stake here between King and Van Dusen and Plato, one first needs to look beyond the complex definitional claims they all make about the meaning of civil disobedience to the question of who has the authority to make such determinations in the first place. For King, divine law licenses the individual to disobey civil law; for Van Dusen divine law is irrelevant in that it is indeterminable and as likely to be invoked by the children of darkness as by the children of light; for Plato, divine law and civil law are inevitably one and the same.

If there is no higher law than the law of the land, Van Dusen's case against civil disobedience is rendered more powerful, King's brief for it is considerably weakened (though not necessarily flattened), and Plato's thoroughgoing rejection of it is, ironically, left hanging by an analogical (family/state) thread. Viewed as a debate over consequences--the explicit tack taken by Van Dusen and Plato, implied in King--civil disobedience can be seen as either the first step down a short, steep and extremely slippery slope to mob violence and chaos or as a civilized means of correcting the law's temporary failure to express those cultural values from which it springs.

In the end, the argument over civil disobedience is an ethical argument; one cannot stand wholly within a system and find a principle by which to either condemn or indemnify that system. One must step beyond the bounds of the system and let history determine whether one was a rebel or a social reformer. In this regard, most certainly Plato's and possibly Van Dusen's cases might be seen as circular. The law cannot condone its own violation; that seems self-evident. And if the law is always right (which in a general sense it is, in that some system of law is essential to human survival), civil disobedience is always wrong.

But what if we start at the other end of the stick? Assume that a law is causing undue suffering to large numbers of people and those people exhaust legal remedies. By definition, what they do next, beyond capitulation and prayer, will be illegal; but it could be right. Unless we grant the latter possibility and frame the question such that it is possible for the law to be wrong, we don't really have an issue. We are back to the argument over the question of how "patient" the victims must be before their case is justified.

CENSORSHIP ON THE INTERNET

- Mike Romano, "In Defense of Decency"
- Kathleen Durkan, "Net Benefit"
- Marc Rothenberg, "The Net Doesn't Need Thought Police"
- Senator James Exon, "Only the Force of Law Can Deter Pornographers"
- James Gleick, "This is Safe Sex?"

As the title makes clear, all of the essays in this unit are engaged in a conversation having to do with censorship on the Internet. They by no means agree either on the facts surrounding recent government efforts to censure the Net nor on their values, with some more concerned about such values as freedom of speech and others more concerned about values related to the protection of children. Interestingly enough, virtually all rely at various points in their arguments upon claims of resemblance (or arguments by precedent), although some may be shown to use the strategy more effectively than others.

Perhaps the best essay to begin with in this unit is Senator Exon's, since all of the arguments on this topic are occasioned to some degree by the recent congressional passage of the Communications Decency Act, a bill that Exon co-sponsored. By beginning with Exon's essay, which is largely a defense of the CDA, students have the opportunity to learn about the law from the horse's mouth, so to speak, and, given the extent to which they find Exon's defense persuasive, gain a more trustworthy understanding of the law than they might expect to gain from any of the other writers. In this matter, in other words, Exon may be credited with having a considerable ethical appeal at the outset that the other writers do not necessarily have.

Exon's is essentially an argument intended to support the claim he makes in his opening paragraph: "Children and families won an important victory in Congress on February 1." The remainder of his essay goes on to explain/argue just how the congressional passage of the bill represents a victory--ultimately, a reasonable step that makes the information superhighway safer and more useful for children and families--and, secondarily, how it does not represent a threat to tradition American freedoms. Not surprisingly, Exon's argument is based largely on the consequences he expects the bill to have, which are implicit in the reasons he offers in support of his claim: the passage of the bill represents a victory 1) because it signifies a step to protect children from pornographers and indecency, 2) because it doesn't violate the First Amendment (i.e., "nothing in it applies to constitutionally protected speech between consenting adults"), 3) because it represents no greater censorship on the Internet as antipornography laws represent for the mail, radio and TV, and phones, 4) because it can be enforced as other existing pornography laws are, and 5) because it can be readily implemented and so achieve its purpose by variety of means, including use of credit cards, debit accounts, and adult identification numbers.

Having outlined the reasons that the CDA represents a victory for children, Exon then goes on in paragraph 16 to anticipate and respond to those opposed to the bill on principle, in the belief that nothing that limits freedom of access to anything by anyone can be good, regardless of the motive for doing so. His response, it should be pointed out, is a good example of a pathetic appeal: "Tell that to a parent who has a child lured away by a deviant on a computer network." After acknowledging that his bill will not end access on the Internet to pornography by children (again, an effective strategy for ethical appeal), he concludes by indulging in a bit of argumentum ad hominem designed to arouse the indignation of his audience by identifying those against the CDA as self-serving elitists who are determined to interpret and defend the Constitution as intended to "make certain that the profiteering pornographer, the pervert, and the pedophile be free to practice their pursuits in the presence of children on a taxpayer created and subsidized computer network."

Time and again, Exon resorts to resemblance arguments (in particular, arguments by precedent) to support his claim, such as when he notes that the CDA, described by Exon as a kind of pornography law itself, "will be enforced in the same way as our existing pornography laws" in paragraph 12, and again, when, in describing the various means by which child access on the Net may be restricted, he points out that "the Supreme Court already has approved such means for limiting child access to telephone 'dial-a-porn' services" in paragraph 13. This strategy is used to even greater advantage in the essay by Romano, who employs it in the context of a broader refutation strategy of the sort described in the context of the assignments provided for Chapters 7 and 8 in the text (see p. 187). Accordingly, Romano's primary purpose seems not so much to be to present an argument in support a particular claim (e.g., censorship of the Internet is ultimately good--although in paragraph 16 at least he certainly does) but rather first to summarize the arguments of those opposing any government effort to censure the Internet and then, one by one, to refute those arguments. An analysis of the strategies that he adopts in the course of his refutation can be especially instructive.

To this end, then, he devotes the opening seven paragraphs to contextualizing the issue inspired by the passage of the CDA and then to summarizing the arguments of those opposed to Internet censorship. As he represents the arguments raised by critics of the CDA, they are essentially three: 1) because all postings on the Internet are equally available to minors as they are to adults, restricting access to children necessarily and unfairly restricts access to adults--that is, in accordance with the findings of the Supreme Court in the matter of <u>Butler v. Michigan</u>, the CDA threatens to reduce the adult population to reading "only what is fit for children"; 2) the CDA's definition of what is "patently offensive" is much too vague; and 3) the "community standards" intended to determine the CDA's indecency levels vary from state to state while the Internet itself knows no boundaries. How then can it be held to any one state's or one community's standards? It should not be lost on students how Romano manages to garner considerable ethical appeal in appearing to represent these arguments objectively and fairly.

With his announcement in paragraph 8 of his intent to respond to the anti-censorship objections, Romano proceeds through paragraphs 9-15 to refute each argument in turn, beginning, appropriately enough, with the first one he mentioned earlier. In paragraphs 9-10, he refutes that objection by demonstrating how a closer reading of the act indicates that it includes provisos ensuring continued access to obscene communications by adults "albeit restricted access," and by using an argument of resemblance to point out the precedent set by previous legislation (<u>FCC v. Pacifica</u>) for ways of restricting access exclusively to children. In paragraph 11, he resorts again to a close reading of the act and to arguments of resemblance to maintain that a second objection "relying heavily on slippery-slope arguments" and consisting of a concern about the phrase "patently offensive" being overly vague and allowing the censorship of even popular art is ultimately groundless insofar as "such reasoning runs contrary to <u>Pacifica</u>" and insofar as it ignores the important qualification that the "patently offensive" material must be such that it can be demonstrated to be <u>intended</u> to be "patently offensive." The third objection Romano refutes in a similar manner in paragraphs 12-15, arguing again on the basis of the precedent represented by the <u>Pacifica</u> ruling and the resemblance to the situation confronted by the broadcast media that concerns about the difficulties posed by the nature of the Internet of adhering to varying "community standards" are needless. As Romano contends, "I fail to see how the Internet is substantively more ubiquitous than radio or television."

Up to this point, Romano's argument represents a solid response to the opposition; indeed if it has a weakness, it might be found beginning in paragraph 15, where he appeals to common experience for support for his denial of the claim that the "Internet has become a last, best chance for democracy." "How many people do you know," he asks, "who actually use the Internet regularly? How many people do you know who have personal Web sites? Let me guess: all of your poor, black, lesbian friends, right?" The answer such questions receive may not be what the writer anticipates. In fact, such appeals are always dangerous for they can easily backfire and border on the fallacious; students may well be prompted to ask just who is the "you" that Romano thinks he is addressing here and to consider whether his assumptions implicit in this appeal are warranted and wise.

Unfortunately, the remaining three essays are considerably weaker than Exon's and Romano's and thus don't add a great deal to the conversation on this issue, although they can serve a useful purpose in the classroom nonetheless. The Gleick essay is helpful to some extent in prompting students to question whether pornography on the Internet poses as great a threat to children as the proponents of the CDA would have us believe. Unfortunately, the relatively few examples Gleick provides in an effort to demonstrate that the threat is minimal are finally insufficient to be adequately convincing. His essay might thus afford an opportunity to discuss with students the limitations of examples as evidence. One contrary example may be sufficient to demonstrate the limitations of a generalization, but one example can hardly serve by itself to establish the legitimacy of a claim. Such is especially the case in those instances such as the one that Gleick is confronting, where the opposition, in this case those who believe the Internet to represent a very real threat to children, is convinced of the inherent rightness of their cause. (Imagine, for example, trying to argue to a convention of dog lovers that dogs make bad pets based upon one or two examples drawn from your own experience. Better yet, have students imagine arguing to a group of fellow students that college is a waste of time and money based solely upon the experience of one or two other students.)

The Durkan essay can be used to provoke students to consider a different kind of problem: just when is an argument an argument, and when is it simply an expression of opinion? In an essay that strives to go beyond the censorship issue proper to contend that there are far greater concerns when it comes to the Internet than concerns about "stamping out smut," Durkan leaves her readers wondering just what her real purpose is and just what she wants them to do or believe. We are informed in the essay about what _her_ concern is, but that's about all; the number of unsubstantiated assertions occurring throughout the piece (such as those she conveys in paragraph 8) render her essay more a mere expression of her opinion than an argument that seems intended to persuade an audience to adopt the stance she does. Finally, we have to ask whether what she says here ultimately compels us to take any stand with regard to some of the matters she raises, or to genuinely care about them.

Last but not least is the Rothenberg piece, which can prove extremely useful, if for no other reason, simply as an example of a flat-out lousy argument. Read in the context of the Exon and Romano essays and in conjunction with Appendix One, this essay will afford students lots of opportunities to locate fallacies of various sorts and, more importantly, to discuss the consequences of their appearance in the argument for the writer's logical, ethical, and pathetic appeals and the persuasiveness of his argument. Faulty analogies, instances of name-calling, slippery slope arguments, unsubstantiated and hasty generalizations as well as other fallacies are all represented here to a degree that even novice readers and writers cannot fail to recognize and decry them. Once acquainted with some of the legitimate terms of the arguments surrounding the issue of censorship and the Internet, students should have fun analyzing the weaknesses in this essay.

Unfortunately, what seems to be lacking in this unit is a genuinely strong argument opposing censorship on the Internet. Instructors might want to take advantage of this state of affairs by challenging their students to construct one of their own.

THE LEGALIZATION OF DRUGS

- Michael Gazzaniga (Interview), "The Federal Drugstore"
- Walter Wink, "Biting the Bullet: The Case for Legalizing Drugs"
- Richard J. Dennis, "The Economics of Legalizing Drugs"
- James Q. Wilson, "Against the Legalization of Drugs"
- Lee N. Robins, Darlene H. Davis, and Donald W. Goodwin, "Drug Use by U.S. Army Enlisted Men in Vietnam: A Follow-Up on Their Return Home"

Although it comes later in this section, we will begin by analyzing the Wilson essay, in large part because of the very clear way it frames and lays out the issue and because of the thoroughness of his coverage.

Wilson begins his essay by looking back to 1972 and his appointment to the Presidential Commission on Drug Abuse Prevention. He thereby simultaneously establishes his <u>bona fides</u> to be speaking on the issue and identifies an historical precedent which will support his view. In making a case for legalizing heroin twenty years ago, Milton Friedman identified two major threads of argument which Wilson will deal with throughout his essay: (1) an argument based on principle which says the government has no right to tell people what not to do even if they might be hurting themselves by doing it; (2) an argument based on consequences which says that the costs of banning drugs outweigh the benefits.

Wilson next asks what might have happened had the Commission followed Friedman's advice. Had heroin been legalized, would heroin usage rates have flattened out and then declined between the early and mid-seventies? Can we doubt for a moment, he asks rhetorically, "that heroin use would have grown exponentially?" In support of his point of view, he cites the Lee Robins study of drug use among returning Vietnam vets which showed that heroin usage (which was quite high in Vietnam) virtually disappeared within a few months of returning home. He attributes this drop to the lack of availability and affordability (which is related to its illegality). [Later, we will see how Gazzaniga interprets the Lee Robins study quite differently.] He in turn scoffs at those who argue that if heroin were more readily available it would hold less appeal to those who currently seek it out as "forbidden fruit." If the price of a Porsche were cut by 95 percent would people lose interest in it? he asks.

To further support his point about the possible effects of legalizing drugs, he turns to Great Britain's experiment in the 60s with increasing heroin availability for addicts. The net result was a thirty-fold increase in addicts. (It's important to notice here that the initial number of addicts was quite low--fewer than 100--so that the expression of the change as a multiple of the original number rather than as a raw number greatly increases the impact.)

He then questions the numbers currently used to estimate how many people might become addicted to cocaine were it legalized. Currently, some 3 percent of all cocaine users develop problems with it. (Part of the confusion over some of the statistics in these essays can be traced to the looseness with which "addiction," "abuse" and "problem" are used without distinguishing the categories from one another.) He argues against extending that ratio into a drug-legalized future for two reasons: 1. it's illogical to assume that you won't increase the percentage of those who abuse it if you make drugs more available; 2. the statistics were gathered before crack--which tends to show higher rates of abuse--was widely used.

In sorting out the costs and benefits of drug legalization, Wilson confronts the oft cited benefit of converting drug tax revenues into enhanced treatment programs for addicts. The more we tax drugs, argues Wilson, the more we raise the price of drugs, thus driving users back toward crime to raise the dollars and making the black market for drugs more likely to flourish. Our inability to find the right equilibrium with alcohol suggests we might well have similar problems with drugs.

In returning to the issue of principle, Wilson suggests that drugs should be illegal because they are immoral. More particularly, he distinguishes cocaine from nicotine on a moral scale, contending that "nicotine alters one's habits, cocaine alters one's soul." Any substance that "destroys the user's essential humanity" is deemed immoral by Wilson.

In his concluding argument, Wilson takes head on the analogy between alcohol and drugs and the suggestion that it is hypocritical to make one legal and the other illegal when they have so much in common. In taking it on, however, he says he will follow neither a strict consequentialist nor a predominantly principled path. He invokes instead "common sense." Alcohol is distinct from drugs first of all because it's not as addictive (an argument he doesn't push because of the difficulties of defining addiction and because of all the non-biological causes that interfere with estimates of a substance's capacity to cause addiction). He chides those who establish the relative benignity of hard drugs by comparing the damage currently caused by drugs to the damage currently caused by alcohol. The proper point of comparison, he says, is the damage caused if both were legal. To compare the effects of an illegal drug whose use is circumscribed by law to a legal one

One-word outline

Department of Philosophy and Religion

PHL1100, Introduction to Philosophy

Winter, 1998

Quiz 1

Name: _____

1. What one, central point do you think Plato is trying to make? (Hint: it is not about immortality.)

that's freely available and widely promoted is sophistry in Wilson's view. And, he asks, if we had to do over again, might we want to keep booze illegal? Could we have saved ourselves much of the undeniable grief it has caused? (Which is to say, he invokes the two wrongs don't make a right argument.)

The last point Wilson makes here is made in the form of a variant of Pascal's Wager: what's to be lost in an unsuccessful experiment versus what's to be lost by wrongly sticking to the status quo. The downside potential for an unsuccessful experiment is, of course, enormous. And frighteningly unknown. The costs of the status quo are well known and, if substantial, acceptable to most. By concluding with this argument, Wilson underscores his considerable rhetorical skill. The most powerful ally of almost any anti-proposal argument is "The devil you know is better than the devil you don't know" principle. To put that case in the last position is to put it in its proper Nestorian Order.

Another comprehensive essay in this group is Michael Gazzaniga's cautious argument, in the form of an interview, for the legalization of drugs. The strength of Gazzaniga's case lies primarily in his careful causal analyses of drug effects. Thus, for example, he begins by dismissing the "hysterical" charge that crack is somehow innately "crimogenic" by asserting that the brain impact of crack and cocaine is the same and that the sort of people who use the two are considerably different because of differences in drug cost. People who smoke crack may commit more crimes, but not because of the drug. To clinch his point, he cites the melodramatic cult film <u>Reefer Madness</u> as a precedent for drug hysteria in our culture. As to the greater addictiveness of crack, he concedes that it probably is, but downplays the degree by pointing to other factors that increase its use, including its cheapness and its special quickness of effect, which tends to keep moderate users away from it. Moreover, he reminds us that there are 300 tobacco related deaths for every one crack related death by way of putting the problem into an amenable perspective. (Here you might point out that Wilson doesn't linger over tobacco related mortality rates, but rather focuses on their effects on character, which pale in comparison.)

The major points of disagreement between Wilson and Gazzaniga, apart from the numerous discrepancies in statistics--which should provide a useful lesson for students in the limits of faith we can place in numbers--concerns the reasons for the relatively level base rate for addiction in recent years. Whereas Wilson, it will be recalled, attributes that levelling of base rate to the continuing sanctions against drug use in America, Gazzaniga attributes it to a sort of "natural phenomenon" and suggests that rates of abuse and addiction would remain constant no matter what. He too cites the Robins study, drawing precisely the opposite conclusion from the one drawn by Wilson. The huge dropoff in drug use among returning vets suggests to Gazzaniga that the base rate of usage will always be returned to after whatever perturbations might make them rise and fall. (He notes, briefly, the lack of data on base rates of addiction from different cultures. Such data might go a long way toward sorting out the truth of the matter in this issue.)

For Gazzaniga, the moral issue is never really addressed. He neither develops the case for the individual's right to use drugs, nor offers an extended refutation of arguments for the immorality of drugs. He focuses on the consequences of drug use and of legalizing drugs and concludes that the benefits outweigh the gains. He downplays the negative effects of drug use and presents an optimistic estimate of science's ability to someday deal with addiction. (Note in this regard that he dismisses the hyperbolic figures on "crack babies" without gainsaying Wilson's contention that between 50,000 and 70,000 babies are annually affected by the fetal drug syndrome.)

Theologian Walter Wink offers a two-pronged attack on the present drug policies by way of arguing in favor of drug legalization. His initial argument, based on principle, is that in committing ourselves to a "war" on drugs, "we become what we hate," a theme he returns to in his conclusion. Most of his argument, however, is taken up with pointing out the negative consequences of the Bush Administration's anti-drug program. Throughout, he offers a series of causal arguments showing the unanticipated negative consequences of each of the three elements of Bush's drug-war.

Bush's attempt to cut off drugs at the source is ineffective because it forces us to rely on foreign governments who are either unwilling or unable to combat the paramilitary drug lords in their midst. Wink invokes the specter/precedent of Vietnam by way of dismissing suggestions to solve the problem by expanding our military presence in these countries. Interdiction hasn't worked and can't work, says Wink. Using sophisticated, expensive equipment has resulted in very few seizures. Moreover, when seizures are made it only results in temporary price escalation; and escalating the price of drugs will increase rather than diminish the worst consequences of drugs in that hardcore addicts will simply steal more to afford their habit.

The major effect of cracking down on dealers and major users has been to overtax our prison system and drive up prison costs dramatically. If fully successful, Bush's strategy would cost nearly two trillion dollars to incarcerate all drug users. Additionally, many Latin American banks would have to default on loans from American banks and drug centers like Miami would lose a huge source of revenue.

For Wink the problem is not drugs so much as drug laws. And the greatest beneficiaries of those laws are the dealers who can charge huge sums for goods not because of production or marketing costs but only because they aren't otherwise legally available. The major victims of those laws are citizens robbed, burgled, or shot by dealers and addicts feeding their habits and protecting their turf.

Wink concludes his argument with a series of claims minimizing the cost and maximizing the benefits of drug legalization. His major claim in all this is that legalizing drugs is the only way to win the war against drugs. Or, to put the matter less oxymoronically, only by legalizing some drugs can we diminish the worst consequences of drugs--crime, enormous cost, and hypocrisy.

In arguing in favor of legalizing drugs, economist Richard Dennis pushes rationality to Swiftian limits. On the whole, though, he argues quite persuasively, laying bare all his assumptions and playing out various scenarios that result from those assumptions in what appears to be a very fair-minded way. What will bother many readers is his persistent reduction of all costs and benefits to dollars and his preemptory dismissal of all non-economic matters. Drugs are "not a moral issue" he says flatly, citing our decision to repeal Prohibition as resolving any moral complications with drug legalization. As a health issue it's small beer and as a societal issue it's overblown. In a word, the problem is money.

But before launching into his economic analysis, Dennis pauses to reassure us that he's not talking about legalizing all drugs for everyone. Children would be prohibited from buying drugs. And any drug more harmful than alcohol would be prohibited. In the absence of moral concern, it's not clear why Dennis is opposed to selling children drugs. (And his comparison to laws about statutory rape are unlikely to clear the matter up.)

Using alcohol as a benchmark for the public's drug-harm tolerance level seems fair, although it's not totally clear how one would determine with any precision if a given illegal drug was more or less harmful than alcohol. And compounding this difficulty are all the environmental conditions that invite people to abuse alcohol and to avoid illegal drugs. If cocaine were legal, readily obtainable and cheap, and if Madison Avenue were making it chic to use it, who is to say how pervasive its ill-effects might become. Moreover, as in all the pro-drug legalization arguments, this line of reasoning is vulnerable to Molly Ivins' First Rule of Holes: "When you're in one, quit digging."

Dennis's boldest argument, one that others tiptoe around in various ways, is his claim that "if reasonable costs are assigned to all aspects of the drug problem, the benefits of drug peace would be large enough to offset even a doubling in the number of addicts." Although his calculus won't work for all, this strategy gets him to where he wants to be--an economic cost-benefit analysis. One wishes he might reveal more of the sources for his estimates, but his care in dealing with those estimates once he has them in hand is impeccable. Assuming that all the warrants undergirding his argument are acceptable, his argument is quite powerful.

Dennis concludes his argument with a laundry list of possible objections to his argument and his rejoinders to those objections. Several points are worth noting here. He argues, for example, that crack ought to remain illegal, which is hard to square with his assertion that government "must make drugs available at all levels of quantity and potency" to prevent development of black markets.

In turn, his notion that legalization of drugs does not imply approval is not persuasively supported. His analogy between legal though offensive drugs and legal though offensive practices such as "atheism, offensive speech, and heavy-metal music" seems wide of the mark. The First Amendment protects all three of his examples as forms of expression; but it would be a stretch to see drug use as a form of expression. And finally, the charge that such a sweeping change could have terrible unforeseen consequences--the Ur anti-proposal argument--is not easy to gainsay. His protest that anything short of total change wouldn't work is less compelling than it is troubling.

In some sense, Dennis's argument could be said to reverse basic Nestorian order, which prescribes the following: second strongest argument first; weakest in the middle; strongest in the conclusion. That is, Dennis places his weakest arguments (or his least well developed arguments at any rate) at the beginning of his essay, his strongest arguments in the middle and his second strongest arguments (and they would appear to be a distant second) in the conclusion in the rhetorically weak form of a list.

We conclude the drug legalization issue with the Robins essay primarily as a model of a scholarly study that provides source material for more popular arguments. While the article itself contains a very carefully developed "argument," it does not itself take a position on the question of drug legalization. As a model argument, the Robins piece is particularly valuable for its transparency. We actually get to see the argument evolve from a concern, to a set of questions, to the development of a methodology for testing answers to those questions, to some carefully drawn conclusions. Wilson and Gazzaniga, on the other hand, are concerned only to borrow Robins's conclusions for their more broad-brushed arguments. And, indeed, one could justifiably draw either Gazzaniga's or Wilson's conclusion from the study.

It is instructive to note the great care with which Robins makes her methodological decisions. Always the goal is to insure that the data will help answer questions central to the study (What was drug usage in Vietnam? What proportion of drug use continued into civilian life? What variables best predicted post-military usage?), and that it was obtained in a way that isolates the proper variables and excludes confounding variables (e.g., insuring that all the subjects were from one branch of service to account for differences in drug programs and experiences among the services.) Her study seems to show conclusively that heroin isn't as addictive as is popularly thought, but why heroin usage declined dramatically once veterans returned home isn't clear. Is it, as Wilson believes, because legal and social stigmas constrain drug usage in the United States? Or is it, as Gazzaniga believes, because the abnormal stress situation of Vietnam led to higher usage levels, which returned to base levels once veterans left the war zone?

SEXUAL HARASSMENT

- Stephanie Riger, "Gender Dilemmas in Sexual Harassment Policies and Procedures"
- Naomi Munson, "Harassment Blues"
- Erica Jong, "Fear of Flirting"
- Gretchen Morgenson, "Watch that Leer, Stifle that Joke"
- Susan Crawford, "A Wink Here, a Leer There: It's Costly"
- Martha Chamallas, "Universal Truth and Multiple Perspectives: Controversies on Sexual Harassment"

The debate over sexual harassment has some interesting parallels to the debate over political correctness that you may want to explore. The place to begin noting parallels lies in the first sentence of Stephanie Riger's essay, where she calls sexual harassment "the most recent form of victimization of women to be redefined as a social rather than a personal problem. . . ." (With both issues, the movement of a concern from the private to the public sphere generates much of the disagreement. For conservatives, codifying campus speech codes and legislating office mores are mostly wrongheaded attempts to intervene in essentially private matters; better to let the putative victims deal with these matters individually as they always have. In both cases, in fact, dealing with the situation is depicted as more character building than debilitating for the victims. And those who complain about their victimization or call for legal support are, by implication, simply not made of stern enough stuff. In some extreme cases, to be sure, public control might be justifiable, but in most cases the obnoxiousness ought to be accepted as a normal part of life. To sum up, in the immortal words of Laker announcer Chick Hearn, "No harm, no foul." For liberals, actions in both cases have palpable and significant negative consequences. College curricula are unnecessarily parochial, minority and female students are prevented from matriculating, women workers are demeaned and stifled, companies lose money, etc. And because of the public consequences of these actions, there ought to be public sanctions against those who perpetrate them. In turn, what is considered normative behavior and speech is not defined according to custom and tradition, but according to values and beliefs not yet fully accepted in the mainstream.)

Concerning the issue of sexual harassment alone, Riger's piece represents the most thorough and scholarly treatment of the issue and focuses on the procedures used to resolve sexual harassment complaints. But to step back for a moment, her point of departure is Gretchen Morgenson's piece which appeared originally in <u>Forbes</u>. Morgenson's contention in that piece is that the concern over sexual harassment is misplaced in that it is a relatively rare occurrence in the workplace.

The misperception that it is widespread, says Morgenson, is the result of a smokescreen being laid by highly paid consultants who profit from offering training advice in how to combat sexual harassment in the workplace. Morgenson's is basically a "conspiracy theory" argument aimed at discrediting these consultants. Her tack is to take quotes from individual consultants who she's apparently interviewed and play them off against statistics gathered by law firms and government agencies that litigate and hear sexual harassment cases. Time and again, the statistics indicate few and declining numbers of complaints and suits, thereby undercutting the consultants' expressions of concern and alarm about the significance of the issue.

In turn, Morgenson criticizes the law for its vagueness. In one instance, she quotes a lawyer who compares our high level of tolerance for "sexual jokes and innuendo" in movies to the low level of tolerance for same exhibited by many complainants. How can men in the workplace possibly know what standard is appropriate when women themselves don't agree what's offensive? Clearly, the whole matter is too full of nuance and subjectivity to become a matter of law.

What the movie analogy misses, however, is the critical disanalogy between theater audiences who voluntarily spend two hours watching movies that are rated according to the potential offensiveness of their content and female workers who must spend 40 hours a week, 50 weeks a year, in the company of fellow employees whose potential to offend is not a matter of public record. An offensive movie is unlikely to retard a moviegoer's career, and seldom will the moviegoer be in an unequal power relationship with other viewers. In the end, it's difficult to see the moviegoer as a potential victim; hence if moviegoers choose, say, to try and get their money back, the burden of proof should properly be on them to show how they've been victimized.

In her rebuttal, Riger takes issue primarily with the validity of Morgenson's statistics as a proper gauge of the seriousness of the problem. Instead of relying on public records, she relies on surveys and studies of the workplace that indicate much higher levels of harassment than those reported in the court records. Instead of assuming in cases of such discrepancies that the legal records are privileged, she argues that "the low rate of utilization of grievance procedures is due to gender bias in sexual harassment policies that discourages their use by women."

From this point on, Riger's argument is essentially a causal one, looking to explain the reasons for so few women reporting or pursuing grievances. In some cases, the causes can be seen as pretty direct (e.g., the chances of winning are slim, the costs of pursuing are high, and the benefits of winning are meager), but in several others, the connection is much more indirect (e.g., women prefer to engage in procedures that result in harmony while men prefer procedures that yield "justice," and present procedures mirror men's preferences quite strongly).

One feature of Riger's argument to have students note carefully is the EEOC guidelines on sexual harassment. In several places throughout other essays, authors play fast and loose with those guidelines. In dealing with those guidelines, Riger makes her most striking claim and one that will almost surely generate a good deal of controversy among students. Riger is positive about the fact that harassment is judged by its effects rather than its intent. However, given that the "reasonable person rule" used to determine how someone would normally respond to a behavior or remark is typically interpreted by males quite differently than it is by females, and given further that those who adjudicate harassment cases are typically male, women rarely get a truly "neutral" hearing. Whereas males are inclined to interpret lewd remarks aimed at women as complimentary, women are inclined to interpret them as insulting. When the final interpretation is left to males, the results, says Riger, will be skewed.

In turning to Munson's argument, we turn to a decidedly more popular treatment of the subject. Her argument is based almost entirely on personal experience reinforced by personal judgments of public sentiment. In her opening, she reports of happy years spent in the randy environs of a news magazine. When one of her colleagues reports a lascivious remark as a case of sexual harassment, she thinks the woman a bit dim. To Munson's then way of thinking, harassment must involve some actual sexual contact. It wasn't until the Hill-Thomas affair that she belatedly realized her own ignorance. Her friend, she concludes, had been right about harassment taking place. (Though her friend's case clearly doesn't meet the EEOC definition of harassment unless it was merely one of many similar incidents; and just as clearly the depiction of Thomas's behavior she provides would meet that definition.)

Munson's standard for judging sexual harassment is finally the prevailing public view. The fact that the public didn't buy Anita Hill's story is for her critical proof that the whole harassment business is a scam. According to Munson, "They [the general populace] know that women have always managed to deal perfectly well with male lust," and that the concern over sexual harassment is an expression of feminist rage at their inability to succeed in the workplace on their own terms. Overlooking the fact that this assumption is not universally shared, what is to be done in those cases where it patently isn't the case that a woman has dealt "perfectly well with male lust?"

Erica Jong's is a more complex version of Munson's argument, recognizing as it does the tensions inherent in a situation where standards of behavior are in flux and where 50 million Frenchmen might in fact be wrong. . . .particularly if the matter in question concerns 50 million French women. While she evinces little sympathy for the "Rape Crisis Commandoes" and the Puritanical self-righteousness that she sees behind the P.C. movement, she has less patience for the Judge Thomases, the Bob Packwoods and the Woody Allens. As she succinctly puts it: "How should we treat these old guys--as antiques or as rapists?"

In the end, she opts for a more merciful judgment. In particular, she argues that we keep separate the matter of men like Bob Packwood's private behavior, which was reprehensible, and his admirable public behavior in support of women's legislation. The public action is more important to Jong than the private behavior, just as issues involving sexual behavior are to her generally less important than issues involving public policy such as rates of pay for women. Indeed her conclusion, which equates the end of sexual inequality with the end of economic inequity, places her much closer to Riger than to Munson.

Attorney Susan Crawford offers a brief economic analysis of the consequences of harassment. In that much of the skepticism about sexual harassment has a decidedly pragmatic bent, her dollars and cents argument might be more effective with the audiences of, say, <u>Forbes</u> than would some of the other more ideologically grounded arguments. Her warrant is something like "Any action which causes a company to lose money is bad" leading to an enthymemic argument like this: "Sexual harassment is bad because it costs Fortune 500 companies $6.7 million." Crawford's economic warrant obviates the need to establish that those claiming harassment are more than whiners. Right or wrong, harassment hurts the bottom line.

Professor Chamallas offers a much more philosophical perspective on the issue, one that harkens back to Stephanie Riger's analysis of sexual harassment. Her basic point is that what passes for "objective" or "universal" truth is simply the predominant view of given time and place. And in harassment cases the privileged viewpoint is that of the defendant, not the victim, a practice she argues for overturning.

In calling for adjudicators to adopt a "victim's perspective" or a "reasonable woman's perspective" and to argue for differential treatment of men and women under the law,

Chamallas will be pushing the envelope for most students. Even students who are sympathetic with her argument may not follow her here on the grounds that men and women aren't that different. (Or to put the matter more formally, her argument might violate the basic Rule of Justice that decrees all members of the same class must be treated in a similar manner.) Some might argue that making victimization an essential element of female identity, legally distinguishing them from males, might even constitute a regressive act. Woman as victim is eerily close, after all, to woman as property, a more traditional view of women's legal status.

RECYCLING AND GARBAGE

- Patricia Poore, "America's 'Garbage Crisis': A Toxic Myth"
- Chris Hendrickson, Lester Lavbe, Francis McMichael, "Time to Dump Recycling?"
- Robert Steuteville, "Don't Dump Recycling"
- Reid Lifset and John Schall, "Response to Hendrickson et al."
- Brenda Platt and Neil Seldman, "Response to Hendrickson et al."
- Lynn Scarlett, "Recycling: Asking the Right Questions"
- Nancy Glaser, "Recylcing: The Other Coast, The Other Story"

Given the extent to which the authors of these arguments rely on hard data and facts, particularly statistics, for their support, and given that the major source of disagreement among them typically concerns the truth of such facts, students would surely benefit from reading this unit in the context of their study of Chapter 6, "Evidence in Argument," and Chapter 8, "Accommodating Your Audience," especially pp. 178-179 on strategies for rebutting evidence. From the various kinds of evidence that the authors employ and from various ways they attack the evidence provided by representatives of an opposing view, students are sure to derive some useful suggestions about strategies to use and strategies to avoid.

Employing an approach to the topic of recycling similar to that adopted by Kathleen Durkan in her approach to the topic of censorship on the Internet in her essay "Net Benefit" discussed above, Patricia Poore chooses to sidestep the matter of whether recycling is good or bad to raise an issue that she thinks is much more important. Concerned that the popular focus on garbage as the problem and recycling as the solution is diverting our attention from more serious environmental issues, Poore takes as her issue question in this essay one that could be phrased this way: "Does our garbage pose a serious environmental problem and does recycling represent the best environmental solution to that problem, as the environmental movement would have us believe?" Her claim in response to that question is no, garbage is not the serious environmental problem we've been led to think it is, and no, recycling is not necessarily the best solution, all for reasons she outlines in paragraphs 2-7: 1) because there are greater environmental hazards out there that truly threaten our lives and our health; 2) because garbage is finally a manageable problem; 3) because recycling is not finally a very economical solution or profitable enterprise; 4) because we don't need recycling to extend the life of landfills; and 5) because we don't need recycling to save resources.

In the course of analyzing her essay, it is possible to point out at least two significant weaknesses. For one, her argument would surely come across as more persuasive were she to have provided more concrete evidence to support her points. As it is, she seems to expect her readers to take many of her assurances simply on faith; students might be encouraged to consider whether she has a right to expect this from the readers she envisions. A second weakness resides in her apparent reluctance to resort to strategies for generating pathetic appeals. Given her acknowledgment of the emotional baggage surrounding the issue of recycling and the psychogical benefit it tends to confer on those who practice it, it would obviously have made sense for her to attempt to respond to those who do see recycling as the way of saving the world by appealing to a far greater degree than she does on pathos. Students might suggest various ways she might have convinced her audience that other environmental threats are far more important than recycling garbage.

What Poore's essay lacks in hard data and concrete evidence, Hendrickson et al.'s essay provides, albeit in support of a somewhat different claim. Accordingly, in an effort to prompt students to appreciate the value of providing specific evidence to support their claims, it would no doubt be worthwhile to ask them at the outset of class discussion to compare the two essays and determine which is more persuasive--our bet is that they'd have little trouble concluding that Hendrickson's is the stronger.

And with good reason, for the Hendrickson essay essentially argues many of the same points as the Poore essay and arrives at many of the same conclusions, but only after providing evidence to justify each conclusion. The authors take as their issue questions in this article two questions that Poore addressed in the course of hers, which they identify in paragraph 4: "Is [recycling] cost effective? Does [recycling] actually preserve resources and benefit the environment?" Significantly, their answers to these questions are the same answers given by Poore, except that here they are presented as conclusions dictated by a careful study rather than as assertions representative of one person's opinion. Thus, in response to the first question, "Is recycling cost effective?" they argue in paragraphs 8-17 that, no, it would appear not to be cost effective, at least in Pittsburgh, once all things are taken into account; landfilling MSW appears substantially less expensive. Nor, as the authors argue in paragraphs 18-24, could recycling be made cost effective were the city to adopt various changes in its current recycling system. In response to the second issue concerning the preservation of resources and the benefit of recycling to the environment, the authors conclude that recycling alone is not the answer, that there are other, more effective strategies that must be undertaken to achieve these two ends: "The long-term answer to managing MSW is likely to include green design, materials choice, component reuse, and incineration, as well as recycling."

Meriting special attention throughout the article is the authors' reliance upon the city of Pittsburgh, a single example, as the basis for most of their conclusions. If students have not already encountered and dealt with the problem elsewhere (see for example our discussion above of the essay by Gleick on the topic of censorship and the Internet), they may benefit here from some discussion designed to alert them to the potential dangers of relying exclusively upon a single example for support of a claim. In particular, they might be encouraged to point out the various ways the authors strive in the essay to legitimize their reliance on Pittsburgh for their conclusions, such as their effort to represent Pittsburgh as a typical Northeastern city "where one would expect waste disposal to be an expensive problem" (paragraph 8), and their effort to anticipate and respond to likely objections from a skeptical audience by acknowledging the "Care must be taken in generalizing from Pittsburgh" (paragraph 16).

As articles written specifically in response to the Hendrickson et al. essay, the next three in this unit afford students the opportunity to observe and compare the effectiveness of a variety of refutation strategies. Students may be asked at the outset to determine which of the three responses they consider the strongest (or the weakest) and why; chances are, their determination will not differ significantly from ours. (As we are fond of telling students, students frequently know more than they think they do, and if given the chance, will prove it.)

In this context, while all three of the responses take issue primarily with the original essay's evidence--that is, all three deny the legitimacy of the facts and statistics Hendrickson et al. rely upon--both the Lifset-Schall and the Platt-Seldman pieces are likely to emerge as contenders for best rebuttal, albeit for different reasons. Lifset and Schall rely for their refutation upon what they argue to be a superior set of data provided by a study of recycling undertaken by the Tellus Institute. Students should be sure to recognize how this strategy of refutation obliges the authors to argue for (not merely assert) the superiority of their data before using it to refute the opposition, a necessary preliminary step that Lifset and Schall are careful to take in paragraphs 2-3. Students should also be asked to take notice of the care with which the authors strive to represent themselves as fair, thoughtful, dispassionate people--of the extent, in other words, to which ethical appeal is especially necessary for an effective refutation--and of the ways in which their dispassionate language and respectful attitude toward their opposition (see the second sentence in paragraph 1) contribute to their credibility and ultimately to the effectiveness of their rebuttal.

The Platt-Seldman piece is equally useful in exemplifying effective strategies for rebuttal, particularly because these authors rely on more than one. In fact, a review of Chapter 6, particularly pp. 133-135, should prompt students to recognize that in the course of their rebuttal these authors attack Hendrickson et al.'s data on the very grounds we claim data to be most susceptible to attack. Thus, in Chapter 6, we encourage students to employ data that is recent, representative, and sufficient: Platt and Seldman's first point of contention criticizes Hendrickson et. al's data for being out of date; the second point attacks the data for being unrepresentative (and hence underscores the dangers of relying upon a single example); the third and fourth points attack the data for being insufficient.

In contrast to the other two, the last response to the Hendrickson article included in this unit, the one by Steuteville, should stand students in good stead as a useful example of what NOT to do in refuting an argument. To initiate discussion, students might be asked to consider just how convincing they find this response, particularly after reviewing the others, and then to identify just what features seem to weaken it. No doubt they will have little difficulty pointing out a variety of flaws, including Steuteville's tendency to reduce the arguments of his opposition to those of a strawman and to respond in emotional language characterized by colloquialisms and slang (e.g., "Whoa" in paragraph 2, and "In fact, the authors' statement comes out of left field" in paragraph 8) that negatively affect his ethical appeal and so ultimately work to diminish his credibility.

The relationship between the last two essays in this unit is similar to the relationship between the first two: the first one by Scarlett introduces the issue and takes a stand on that issue, but largely ignores the burden of proof; the second one by Glaser responds to the same issue and even takes a similar stand but, more importantly, provides the concrete evidence in support of that stand that ultimately makes her argument considerably more persuasive. Again, taken together, the pair affords students a useful opportunity to compare the consequences of supporting or not supporting one's claims.

Read in the context of the preceding five articles, Scarlett's revision of the issue-question and the stance she takes on it seem almost natural and inevitable, an impression that may lead some students to deny that her lack of supporting evidence is a serious flaw. As she redefines it in paragraph 4, the issue question becomes, "not 'Is recycling good or bad?'" but rather, "How do we best ensure efficient (conserving) use of resources?" The answer representing her stance on this issue is a simple one amounting essentially to the last sentence in her essay: "What makes sense depends on the material, the product, the process, and local circumstance." Significantly, it is an answer that many readers of the previous articles will find it easy to assent to, a phenomenon that may, assuming Scarlett is depending for her audience on those already very familiar with recent conversations on recycling, excuse her for providing what little evidence she does. Needless to say, this essay could easily foster a very productive discussion about just how one's intended audience and their familiarity with the conversation surrounding one's argument can affect and can be assumed to affect the nature and the extent of the evidence needed to persuade them.

Of course Scarlett's reference to Seattle, a state she claims that combatants in the debate over recycling could learn a lot from, forms a perfect segue into the last article in this series by Nancy Glaser. In its focus on a single city, Glaser's article also serves as a perfect companion piece to the article on Pittsburgh by Hendrickson et al. ; while the Hendrickson piece serves to suggest on the basis of one city that recycling does not work, the Glaser piece works to suggest, again on the basis primarily of one city's experience, that recycling can and does work. Accordingly, a comparative analysis of the two essays in terms of the nature and the effectiveness of their various persuasive strategies is sure to be a productive exercise. Another useful exercise might be to have students follow the positive examples of refutation provided by the Lifset-Schall and Platt-Seldman in their attack of the Hendrickson article and imagine how they might (legitimately) refute the arguments put forth by Glaser; or, following the negative example offered by Steuteville, they might be asked to construct a similarly flawed rebuttal of Glaser and to be prepared to point out just what those flaws are and how they imagine they would work to diminish the argument's effectiveness.

SOCIAL POLICY TOWARD THE HOMELESS MENTALLY ILL

- Paul S. Appelbaum, "Crazy in the Streets"
- Jonathan Kozol, "Are the Homeless Crazy?"
- Steven Vanderstaay, "The Homeless Mentally Ill"
- E. Torrey Fuller, "Who Goes Homeless?"

[See also, Charles Krauthammer's "How to Save the Homeless Mentally Ill" in Chapter 10 and Stephen Bean's "What Should Be Done about the Mentally Ill Homeless?" in Chapter 14]

The homelessness issue is an excellent one to help students understand the complexities of arguing with data. The estimates of the numbers of homeless people and the composition of that population vary significantly, as do the research methods used to arrive at those figures. But it is important not to let the numbers dominate the debate; even assuming that the quantitative issues were resolved, a number of important ideological differences would remain. Indeed the homelessness issue is a useful barometer for measuring shifts in American political philosophy and the subsequent effects of those shifts on the American populace over the past thirty years. (While less directly related to sexual harassment issues, homelessness is not unrelated, particularly in the sphere of public responsibilities and private autonomy and the line between those two spheres.)

Appelbaum's essay is essentially a causal argument, laying out the major reasons why deinstitutionalization of mental patients occurred and in turn why that policy is so difficult to reverse even when its failures are palpable. He uses historical analysis to establish the first set of causes, and political analysis to establish the second set. In his first analysis, Appelbaum traces the evolution (or devolution) of deinstitutionalization through roughly half a dozen stages over a period of twenty years. By tracing it through so many discrete stages and acknowledging the many causes for its development, Appelbaum helps us understand just how such an apparently catastrophic movement could develop so much momentum.

The major causes for deinstitutionalization cited by Appelbaum include: (1) the conviction of younger psychiatrists involved in the treatment of WW II troops that traditional forms of treatment, centering on long term institutionalization, were ineffective; (2) the development of Thorazine, a drug which controlled the most pathological symptoms of psychotic disorder, thereby rendering severely mentally ill persons "safe"; (3) the influential work of Erving Goffman who convinced many that institutionalization was itself the cause of many patients' psychiatric problems (cf. Kozol's reversal of this causal explanation--that deinstitutionalization is the cause of many homeless people's mental disorders); (4) the shift in federal policy which called for states to develop community health centers, and which initiated the shift from state to federal control of mental health policy; (5) the prevailing arguments of civil libertarian lawyers "fresh from victories in the civil-rights movement," that the rights of the individual took precedence over the individual's mental health needs; (6) the influential work of psychiatrists like Szasz and Laing who argued that mental illness was a mechanism for social control more than pathology; and (7) the vision of huge dollar savings on the part of states hoping to close their mental hospitals down.

So compelling were these forces that no one appears to have done any serious research into the effects of deinstitutionalization until well after most patients were out the door. The growing awareness of the homelessness phenomenon now makes clear, Appelbaum notes, that the policy has not been very effective. While many former hospital patients were simply shifted into nursing homes, Appelbaum contends that "between 40 and 60 percent of homeless persons" are former mental patients. [Note, though, that Kozol argues that these persons went first into low-cost housing and ended up on the streets only when economic changes including gentrification of cities eliminated most of the nation's single-occupancy boarding houses.]

What a study of this population makes clear, says Appelbaum, is that the behaviors once attributed by Goffman to "institutionalism" are in fact "the effects of the underlying psychiatric illness." And, by the same token, the individual autonomy sought for these patients by civil-rights lawyers appears to be mainly illusory. And, finally, even the hopes of saving money have been dashed by the realities of the political budgeting process. Having said all that, why hasn't the process been reversed? According to Appelbaum, this paralysis stems from "the transformation of deinstitutionalization from a pragmatic enterprise to an ideological crusade." Freedom from institutional control became an end in itself; the virtues of benevolence got confused with the evils of paternalism. By scrupulously guarding the rights of the homeless, we freed ourselves of the obligation to help the homeless.

This "ideological" explanation for inaction may not satisfy all readers, particularly those who don't agree with Appelbaum's contention that nearly 60 percent of the homeless are mentally ill. Clearly, economic factors, such as recession, growing structural unemployment and chronic underemployment, dwindling state tax bases and monolithic voter opposition to taxes, all of which get short shrift in this argument, have something to do with the lack of a strong governmental response. And indeed, to generations raised on The Titticut Follies and One Flew Over the Cuckoo's Nest, there may well be lingering doubts about the efficacy of institutional solutions to mental illness. Still, it is an explanation that resonates with several other explanations offered for other phenomena in these pages.

Kozol takes issue indirectly with Appelbaum's analysis first by disputing that a majority of the homeless are in fact former mental patients, and second by offering some very different solutions to the problem based on his conclusion about the composition of the homeless population. Kozol's argument too is primarily causal in nature. But, taking his initial evidence from the experiences of those who work with the homeless rather than from historical analysis, Kozol identifies the basic problem as "the lack of homes and of the income with which to rent or acquire them." In turn, the causes of this situation include (1) the dramatic loss of jobs offering more than poverty wages; (2) the drop in welfare benefits for families with children; (3) the loss of low income housing to urban gentrification; and (4) the loss of federal support for low income housing production.

While acknowledging that significant numbers of the homeless are indeed mentally ill, Kozol points out that a majority of the homeless in New York (here presumed to be typical) are either children or the parents of children, both groups of which are too young to have been refugees from mental institutions. Far more persuasive to Kozol are the statistics showing that low income housing has practically vanished. Moreover, to the extent that homeless people are mentally disturbed, their homeless condition must surely contribute to their symptoms, argues Kozol, given their vulnerability and the stresses associated with street life. Indeed, for Kozol, the denials and self-deceptions exhibited by the mentally ill are more prevalent among politicians declaring the problem solved than among the homeless.

Vanderstaay's argument is essentially an extension of Kozol's argument. Its first point of focus is on the "myth" of deinstitutionalization as the cause of homelessness. Here, Vanderstaay offers a more complete argument for severing the link between deinstitutionalization in the 50s and 60s and homelessness in the 80s and 90s. In turn, Vanderstaay offers a fuller argument for reversing the causal direction between homelessness and mental illness. Using testimony from both victims and professionals who treat them, Vanderstaay makes a plausible case for homelessness causing mental illness. One interesting note sounded in conjunction with this causal argument is the contention by Dr. Anne Braden Johnson that "the detachment prized by science has allowed researchers to look at specimen homeless people so objectively that the possibility of their having been driven mad by worry, fear, grief, guilt, or shame has not seriously entered the observers' minds." The idea that "objectivity" is less than an ideal way of looking at the world is a leitmotif throughout these arguments and you might wish to expand on this issue with students.

For Vanderstaay, the more immediate cause of homelessness and in turn mental illness is economic decline. Poverty is the underlying social issue and consequently any attempt to deal with homelessness that ignores structural unemployment and the newly emergent abyss between the haves and the havenots in our society is doomed. For Vanderstaay, job training and education are much more critical tools in combatting homelessness and mental illness than are mental institutions and medications.

Torrey's statistical analysis is more developed than either Kozol's or Appelbaum's. He not only offers an estimate of homeless people (300,000-400,000), he shows us how he arrived at the figure. This estimate is down considerably from early estimates; at the same time, tolerance for the homeless is also going down. Torrey suggests that there is a "growing consensus" about the types of people who are homeless, and he divides them into three groups: families, mentally ill, and alcoholics and drug abusers. The mentally ill comprise approximately one-third of this group, or slightly more than 100,000 in absolute numbers. For Torrey, this group presents the easiest problem to solve. The key to knowing how to solve the problem rests on our ability to recognize its cause.

Here, Torrey offers a brief historic analysis, showing how the fiscal burden for dealing with mental illness has shifted from the states to the federal government. While not in itself a problem, the states now have numerous incentives for discharging mental patients who can be moved over to federal programs like medicaid should they relapse. But the states save money by getting them out of the institution and have no reason to follow up on their care. The solution, Torrey suggests, is to "meld state and federal funding streams" and to make states, who are at the source of the problem, responsible for solving the problem. The states would now have an incentive to avoid costly rehospitalization for which they would bear partial responsibility. Torrey's essay, it should be noted, is the only one of the first three that offers a full blown solution to the problems of the homeless mentally ill.

[Note: Torrey's essay offers teachers an opportunity to help students learn something about government funding. In our experience, students have little sense of the differences among income taxes, sales taxes, property taxes, and so forth as well as little sense about what levels of government are responsible for what activities and services. When Charles Krauthammer, for example, proposes a cap on the mortgage interest deduction to fund the rebuilding of asylums, most of our students have no idea what he means. They are equally confused by Torrey's discussion of state versus federal funding streams. It is useful, we think, to provide students a crash civics lesson in the realpolitik of government funding.]

SAME-SEX MARRIAGE

- Andrew Sullivan, "Here Comes the Groom: A (Conservative) Case for Gay Marriage"
- Dennis O'Brien, "Against Gay Marriage--I: What Heterosexuality Means"
- John Leo, "Gay Rights, Gay Marriages"
- Jonathan Rauch, "For Better or Worse? The Case for Gay (and Straight) Marriage"

The conversation represented by the four essays in this unit provides students with a useful opportunity to observe disagreements among the disputants occurring not so much at the level of fact, as they did for example in the conversation among the writers included in the unit on garbage and recycling, but rather at the level of values and beliefs. Initiating this conversation is an article by Andrew Sullivan who takes as his issue the question, Should civil gay marriage be legalized? His answer is that it should be legalized, albeit the reasons he offers in support of his position seem to all run together, making them difficult at times to isolate and distinguish. But before leading students on a search for those reasons, it might be worthwhile, even at this point, to call their attention to the way in which Sullivan has qualified his claim; if asked, some students will no doubt oversimplify it to something like, Should gay marriage be allowed? thereby omitting the important qualification that Sullivan has been careful to stipulate, that he is arguing for the civil recognition of gay partnerships. Other kinds of recognition he leaves alone, a decision students might be asked to explain and evaluate in assessing the strengths and weaknesses of his argument.

The reasons Sullivan offers for legalizing civil gay marriage are derived mainly from arguments of consequence, and, as they are presented in paragraphs 9, 10, and 11, appear to include the following: 1) because gay marriage has advantages over the present domestic partnership arrangements in that it would a) provide civil recognition of gay relationships, b) would not permit unmarried heterosexuals to qualify for benefits and entitlements, and c) would maintain the traditional meaning and prestige of marriage as a social institution designed to promote stability and security--that is, in short, civil gay marriage should be legalized because the present domestic partnership arrangement is unsatisfactory; 2) because legalizing gay marriage would "offer homosexuals the same deal society now offers heterosexuals," including, "general social approval and specific legal advantages in exchange for a deeper and harder-to-extract-yourself-from commitment to another human being" (paragraph 11), as well as "social cohesion, emotional security, ... economic prudence," and an environment in which to nurture children; 3) because legalizing gay marriage would "reinforce a healthy social trend"; 4) because legalizing gay marriage would signify a public health measure against AIDS. Additional reasons are provided in paragraph 14: legalizing gay marriage would be "good for gays" in providing role models for gay youth and in bridging the gulf between gays and their straight families.

Paragraphs 12 and 13 Sullivan devotes to rebutting opposing views, particularly the view that holds that legalizing gay marriage would work to delegitimize straight marriage and threaten heterosexuality. In both cases, Sullivan relies upon a strategy of refutation derived from logical appeal and demonstrates that such views are based upon logical inconsistencies and fallacies.

When asked to assess the strengths and weaknesses of Sullivan's argument, students are likely to point to the difficulties they had discerning each of Sullivan's reasons, and they should. They might also note how few of his assertions concerning the effects he believes legalizing civil gay marriage <u>could</u> have are actually supported, and so might engage in some discussion about how necessary such support is for Sullivan to make a convincing argument and just what form such supporting evidence could have possibly taken. A case in point is his (seeming) reliance on mere guesswork, first to establish that a majority of gays today, in contrast to the rebels of 20 years ago, are ready to take advantage of the sense of belonging that marriage represents (paragraph 8), and again to establish that most gays would embrace the opportunity marriage would afford them to serve as role models for gay youth. Of course, the fact that Sullivan is himself gay, a fact not revealed in the article itself and one probably unknown to most students at least until they encounter the third article in this unit by Leo, complicates this issue considerably. It is surely worthwhile to invite students to consider, first, whether, not knowing Sullivan's status as a gay male, they find this reliance on guesswork at all problematic and then, upon learning Sullivan's identity as a gay person, to what degree that identity lends his guesswork an authority that it might not otherwise have.

If your students identify as another weakness in the argument Sullivan's failure to antipate and respond to those who might oppose his notion that "Since there's no reason gays should not be allowed to adopt or be foster parents, [legalizing gay marriage] could also help nurture children" (paragraph 11), they will be well prepared to encounter the next two arguments in this unit, both of which point to matters related to the procreation of children in arguing against gay marriage.

Students are likely to find the O'Brien essay a tough row to hoe, and again, we would suggest engaging them in a discussion to determine why. All too often students take the responsibility upon themselves when communication breaks down, automatically assuming that, as readers, the fault is theirs rather than the writer's. As a result, they may be reluctant to point out flaws in others' writing, especially writing that appears in print, believing that to try to do so can only result in an embarrassing revelation of their own ignorance. Obviously, such reluctance is especially dangerous to a democracy, and equally detrimental to the classroom as well, where, according to the same logic, students' first impulse may be to blame their instructors as their readers for failing to understand what they were saying as writers when the fault for a breakdown in communication may in fact be finally theirs. In any event, we try to encourage students to feel free to acknowledge problems a particular reading posed for them and in analyzing the reasons for those problems, to recognize that communication is a responsibility that readers and writers share.

In part, the difficulties posed by the O'Brien piece are a function of simple vagueness--references to ideas, people, and texts that students are unlikely to be acquainted with, embedded in the context of an argument carried on at a relatively high level of abstraction. Just what does O'Brien mean, for example, in paragraph 11 which begins, "I would like to believe that sex is a human artifact for all that it has a biological base . . . " or, in his penulatimate sentence, which reads "In so far as these Judaic faiths are not finally enacted in the realm of attitudes, they seem destined to give a special place to embodiment"? In speculating about the sources of such vagueness, students may conclude one source to be O'Brien's assumptions about his audience; in writing for a particular publication, <u>Commonweal</u>, O'Brien clearly has license to make certain assumptions about that audience and their familiarity with the conversation he is participating in, based upon the readership the publication is known to attract. Any vagueness emerging in his article for a "lay"audience or one that he does not necessarily have in mind may or may not be excused, and again may provoke students to consider the value of context in determining the strengths and weaknesses of an argument.

At the same time, there may be other sources of vagueness in the article, not the least of which may be some uncertainty on the part of the writer himself of just what he wants to accomplish here. It can be very difficult to argue any case if one isn't sure where one stands on the issue and what the chances are of being able to argue it persuasively and successfully. O'Brien's article begins with an admission that "My firmest conviction on this debate [of gay marriage] is that it will end up with no conviction"--testimony which could be interpreted to signify the writer's belief in the futility of arguing the issue in the first place. That belief may in fact be responsible for the impression the article gives of the writer working his way through a problem he's curious to explore, asking himself questions and thinking it through as he writes, with an eye not so much toward finally persuading an audience, but rather toward discovering with them some of the matters to be considered in making an argument on the issue, matters that would seem to lead, finally, to the discovery of a defensible claim.

Even the most novice readers should be able to discern what that claim finally is: the writer is against gay marriage (the title says as much), and bases his opposition in large part on religious tradition--in essence, gays cannot, should not be allowed to marry because their inablity to procreate prevents them from supporting the legal, political, and most importantly the religious values that marriage represents.

In John Leo's article, students again encounter arguments against gay marriage, albeit Leo makes his case without resorting to religious tradition and does so in a much more accessible article. In short, his claim is that gay marriage should not be legalized. After acknowledging the traditional argument in favor of legalization ("Society ought to sanction almost any arrangement that promotes personal commitment and social stability"--his silence on this argument goes along distance toward suggesting a sympathy to it), he proceeds to present his reasons, arguing that gay marriage should not be legalized 1) because marriage is intended to privilege those capable of having children, which gays are not; 2) because domestic partner legislation already ensures many of the benefits conferred on married couples; 3) because permitting gay marriage would "profoundly" alter "a conception of marriage that goes back thousands of years" with possibly dire effects; 4) and because polls indicate that most Americans are opposed to it but willing to accept some legislation giving gays "spousal rights."

Worth discussing in the context of any consideration of this article's strengths and weaknesses as an argument is the degree to which the rhetorical situation has affected the writer's choices, particularly concerning matters of evidence and support, and the extent to which the demands of that rhetorical situation can and should be taken into account in evaluating the argument. To this end, students should be encouraged to discover any clues that suggest Leo's ultimate purpose in this article (just how determined is he to change his readers' minds?), such as the relative brevity of the article itself as well as the brevity of the individual paragraphs, and then invited to compare it to one of the more formal, sustained arguments presented in this anthology (the article that concludes this unit would be a good choice).

More developed than any of the previous arguments in this unit, Rauch's article affords students probably the best example of a model argument in the series. Ideally, students themselves will have already voiced a suspicion that the reliance of the previous two articles on the fact that gays cannot have children has rendered them vulnerable to attacks such as those Rauch carries out. No doubt some have already objected to the claim made by O'Brien and to an even greater extent by Leo that procreation is a critical criterion for marriage by pointing out that many couples marry today with no intention of having children, while many gay couples are certainly capable of "having," that is, raising, children if not of procreating. If so, they are sure to take some pleasure in seeing their objections echoed here.

Rauch begins his argument as a rebuttal, and by doing so in such a way as to take issue with both sides of the debate ("both sides are wrong"), strives to gain a hearing from both sides and so make room for his own position. Taking the debate out of any religious context, Rauch confines his argument to "the world of secular law and policy" and so characterizes the two extreme sides of the debate as the gay side and the traditionalist side. The gay argument, he claims, amounts to belief that "marriage is for love, and we love each other, therefore we should be able to marry." The traditionalist argument he represents as, "marriage is for children, and homosexuals do not (or should not) have children, therefore you should not be able to marry." After refuting the gay side by arguing that love is not <u>the</u> defining characteristic of secular marriage (paragraphs 4-7), he turns to refute in paragraphs 8-14 , not the argument of the other extreme, the traditionalists, but an argument against gay marriage that he characterizes as "Hayekian," the argument that "marriage is as it is and should not be tampered with." Only after he has demonstrated the problems inherent in the Hayekian position does he address at some length (paragraphs 15-33) those that he earlier characterized as tradional.

Of special interest of course will be the strategies Rauch employs to refute the various opposing views he acknowledges; accordingly, this a good essay to discuss in the context of a study of Chapter 8 of the text. In particular, students should notice the extent to which Rauch relies for his refutation on demonstrations of the ways that arguments of the opposition are logically flawed and internally inconsistent, for which purpose he frequently calls upon arguments of definition and resemblance, especially precedent. Arguments developed from definition and from precedent, for example, enable him to establish that, contrary to what many gay activists would argue, love is not now nor has it ever been <u>the</u> defining characteristic of marriage as an institution. Using arguments of resemblance, he refutes the Hayekian view that prohibiting gay marriage represents merely a "trivial disenfranchisement" by likening the prohibition to the one that once made it illegal for blacks to marry whites. To rebut the Hayekian claim that gay marriage should be prohibited because legalizing it might have negative consequences, Rauch cites the example of the legalization of contraception: "Bad things happened as a result of legalizing contraception, but that did not make it the wrong thing to do" (paragraph 13). An expecially good example of Rauch's effort to refute an opposing view by demonstrating its logical flaws can be found in paragraphs 19-25, in his response to Hadley Arkes' claim that the concept of marriage depends upon the anatomical possibility that the two partners can procreate.

FAMILY VALUES, SINGLE PARENTHOOD, AND WELFARE REFORM

- Katha Pollitt, "Why I Hate 'Family Values' (Let Me Count the Ways)"
- Elijah Anderson, "Abolishing Welfare Won't Stop Poverty, Illegitimacy"
- Barbara Dafoe Whitehead, "Dan Quayle was Right"

[See also Charles Murray's essay in Chapter 2 along with various responses and reactions]

The so-called family values debate has continued to capture national attention primarily because of structural changes in our society and our economy which have left many Americans confused about the values they grew up with. Married couples either can't afford or don't desire the more traditional one-income family model. Those with children may find their economic aspirations (or simply their economic survival) to be in conflict with their parental obligations and expectations. Those who are in the second or third generation of impoverishment may view traditional values (if they view them at all) as irrelevant to their circumstances entirely.

The catalyst for the most recent avatar of the debate (which has gone on in many forms for many years) was Dan Quayle's election-year speech on "restoring basic values." It might be useful, therefore, to provide students with some background on that speech as a context for understanding some of the issues raised by the essays in this unit. Specifically, Quayle responds in that speech to questions raised by the Japanese about the causes of the Los Angeles riots of 1992 and who was to blame. His response: "In a nutshell: I believe the lawless social anarchy which we saw is directly related to the breakdown of family structure."

In his speech, Quayle goes on to identify the culprit as a breakdown in "nurture" rather than in "nature," and in doing so implies that government might play a role in solving the problem. And Quayle does have a role in mind for government, though it's not the sort of government intervention that liberals typically prescribe. Scripture, Quayle reminds us, tells us that "The poor you always have with you." However, he's quick to add, today's poor are a different sort--they comprise something called an "underclass."

One key to this debate hinges, then, on our acceptance or rejection of the definition of the underclass as a unique phenomenon. (In exploring this issue further, you might wish to refer to Stephanie Coontz' The Way We Never Were, a book which calls into question the uniqueness both of today's underclass as well as today's middle class.) Only if today's poor are different "in kind" from yesterday's poor, are the radical sorts of solutions called for by Charles Murray (who coined the phrase for contemporary usage) justifiable (see Murray's essay, "The Coming White Underclass," in Chapter 2).

The primary features of this new underclass include high illegitimacy rates, lack of two-parent families, chronic unemployment, and violence. And race: most are black, except that Murray argues that a white underclass is about to emerge now that the rate of white illegitimacy is reaching a critical mass. The underlying cause of the underclass problem, as Quayle argues in his speech, is an absence of values; in turn, Quayle's solution involves changing the "basic rules of society in our inner cities." Among these changes, Quayle includes a reemphasis on law and order, a program that offers home ownership opportunities to the poor, the creation of "enterprise zones" (i.e. lowering business and corporate taxes) in inner cities, a reemphasis on academic standards in public schools, development of a school voucher program, and reforming welfare programs so as to penalize failures to adhere to traditional values. Not surprisingly, most of these solutions involve either less revenue being collected by the government or fewer dollars being disbursed by the government.

It is in his conclusion that Quayle makes even more controversial claims. After skewering Murphy Brown for offering a faulty role model to the underclass, Quayle goes on in his speech to suggest that we return to a "public commitment to our Judeo-Christian ethic." The warrant for this reemphasis apparently requires no backing, for none is offered; after all, "most of us in this room know that some things are good, and other things are wrong."

It's this last portion of Quayle's argument that Pollitt picks up on, labelling Quayle's proposal a variant of "the trickle-down theory of values." She firmly rejects Quayle's assumption about the self-evident superiority of the nuclear family unit (in cases where spouse abuse is prevalent, is keeping the family intact more important than keeping it safe?), and asks what alternatives women facing single motherhood have (abortion?) which aren't more objectionable to the right than raising the child alone. In her response, Pollitt counters the suggestion that single motherhood is a preference and emphasizes the extent to which it is a consequence of limited choices.

If young women of the "underclass" had more options and more hope, they might make happier choices; and if young men had better sex educations, they might not force the choice in the first place. In the end, drawing on personal experience with her recent marital separation, Pollitt points up some of the advantages of single parenthood and suggests that if men accepted a greater share of responsibility for their children, most of the negatives associated with it (e.g., poverty and lack of male role models) would evaporate.

For Pollitt, our failure lies not in our inability to adhere to traditional values, but in our failure to adapt those values to contemporary realities. Divorced women with children are doomed to poverty only to the extent that women are not paid equitably to men. In this case, one maladaptive value--gender bias--reinforces another--stay married no matter what. If women were recognized as equal members of the work force, and if child support laws were properly enforced, single parenting would become a viable option in Pollitt's eyes. For Pollitt, all the fuss about family is not about values, "it's a problem of money." The family values proponents, meanwhile, are simply "bashing" women, particularly poor ones, unfairly. And, following Samuel Johnson, she argues that marriage is not a natural or privileged state; as evidenced by all the constraints and incentives society vainly attaches to it, it appears to be quite an unnatural one.

Sociologist Elijah Anderson, meanwhile, focuses in more directly on the money issue, particularly the welfare system. Specifically, he takes issue with Charles Murray's causal argument against welfare on the grounds that it encourages illegitimate births. According to Anderson's counter-argument, the financial incentives for inner-city women to have children are far less important than other factors. For example, inner city males prey on younger inner city females in order to display their sexual prowess, says Anderson. And this "game" is all important to these young men precisely because they have few other sources of self-esteem. Moreover, the changes in the newly emerging global economy tend to be structural rather than cyclic, and inner-city residents haven't got the education or skills to compete in that economy. This economic crisis in turn creates a sense of hopelessness that makes possibility of normal family life seem very remote to young people. To do away with welfare would, in Anderson's view, simply increase this sense of hopelessness and cause more, not fewer, illegitimate births.

With Barbara Dafoe Whitehead's article, we shift from a focus on the "underclass" to a broader focus on the effects of divorce on all children. Her first major point is that divorce has considerable negative impact on children, and she spends much of the article quantifying and discussing those impacts. Her second major point is that we have historically backed away from a full acknowledgement of these negative impacts, fearing the racist or sexist overtones of such acknowledgement. Both then are essentially causal claims; the second claim, because of the qualitative nature of the judgment is harder to establish.

As Whitehead poses the problem, we are today faced with the following question: "How do we begin to reconcile our long-standing belief in equality and diversity with an impressive body of evidence that suggests that not all family structures produce equal outcomes for children?" During the post-war period, Whitehead argues, as divorce became ever less stigmatized, there was a shift in priorities from children's welfare to adults' happiness. (It's interesting to note all the different places Whitehead explores for the grounds of her argument. She looks to TV shows, greeting cards, popular magazines, college textbooks and kids' books as well as traditional scholarly sources. Students may well be surprised to find a "serious" writer relying so heavily on "popular" sources such as these. Insofar as students are often more familiar with such sources than with traditional sources, they might be more comfortable with them and better able to negotiate them.)

Much of Whitehead's argument is spent identifying and quantifying all the different negative impacts of single parent families. In the face of the staggering number of impacts and the plethora of evidence, students might forget to ask some critical questions. In particular, as Whitehead acknowledges toward the end her essay, there are some lingering questions about the direction of causality and the role that divorce plays in all the impacts noted. Only one of the studies she cites, for example, explicitly "disaggregates the data" in such a way that allows the authors to conclude that divorce causes poverty more than poverty causes divorce. In light of Anderson's argument, which attributes many of the dysfunctions of inner city life to poverty, that's an important discrimination. While Whitehead offers testimony to the effect that the two-parent family structure is preferable, there is less conclusive evidence for the direction of causality.

VI. SELECTED BIBLIOGRAPHY OF WORKS ON ARGUMENT

D'Angelo, Frank J. A Conceptual Theory of Rhetoric. Cambridge, MA: Winthrop, 1975. [Theorizes that linguistic structures, including formal paradigms, match innate conceptual structures of cognition.]

⎯⎯⎯⎯. "Paradigms as Structural Counterparts of Topoi." In Linguistics, Stylistics, and the Teaching of English Composition. Ed. Donald McQuade. (Akron, OH: U. of Akron Department of English, 1979.) [Influenced our sense of form as a heuristic: formal paradigms, analogous to the classical topoi, guide invention and arrangement.]

Berthoff, Ann E. Forming/Thinking/Writing: The Composing Imagination. Rochelle Park, NJ: Hayden, 1978. [Influenced our view of the "new rhetoric"; stresses writing as a process of making meaning.]

Browne, M. Neil, and Stuart M. Keeley. Asking the Right Questions: A Guide to Critical Thinking. 4th ed. Englewood Cliffs, NJ: Prentice Hall, 1994. [Contains useful guide questions, strategies, examples, and exercises to help students learn how to analyze and evaluate arguments.]

Bruffee, Kenneth A. A Short Course in Writing. 2nd ed. Cambridge, MA: Winthrop, 1980. [Uses various four-paragraph shapes as heuristics; gives practical advice o n collaborative learning.]

Cooper, Sheila, and Rosemary Patton. Writing Logically, Thinking Critically. 2nd ed. New York: Longman, 1997. [A useful resource for examples and exercises that encourage critical thinking and the development of effective arguments.]

Corbett, Edward P.J. Classical Rhetoric for the Modern Student. 1965; 2nd ed. New York: Oxford UP, 1971. [Comprehensive introduction to classical conceptions of argument.]

Elbow, Peter. Writing Without Teachers. New York: Oxford UP, 1973. [Influenced our view of freewriting and introduced us to the "believing / doubting game."]

Fahnestock, Jeanne, and Marie Secor, "Teaching Argument: A Theory of Types." CCC 34 (February 1983): 20-30. [Rationale for approaching argument through the stases or modes.]

Fulkerson, Richard, "Technical Logic, Comp-Logic, and the Teaching of Writing." CCC 39 (1988): 436-52. [Strong critique of traditional textbook methods of teaching argumentation, especially their confused and confusing explanations of induction and deduction and formal logic.]

Fulwiler, Toby, and Art Young, eds. Language Connections: Writing and Reading Across the Curriculum. Urbana, IL: NCTE, 1982. [Helped form our views on the value of expressive writing.]

Gage, John T. "An Adequate Epistemology for Composition: Classical and Modern Perspectives." In Essays on Classical Rhetoric and Modern Discourse. Eds. Robert J. Connors, Lisa S. Ede, and Andrea A. Lunsford. Carbondale, IL: Southern Illinois UP, 1984. [Argues that an awareness of audience precedes purpose; the dividing issue is not "the rhetor's invention" but "the outcome of his presence in a conflict of belief."]

_____. "Teaching the Enthymeme: Invention and Arrangement." Rhetoric Review 2 (September 1983): 38-50. [Reveals the enthymeme as a powerful heuristic and shaping device.]

Hillocks, George Jr., Elizabeth A. Kahn, and Larry R. Johannessen. "Teaching Defining Strategies as a Mode of Inquiry: Some Effects on Student Writing." RTE 17 (October 1983): 275-84. [Presents empirical evidence in support of hypothesis that teaching systematic defining strategies leads to cognitive growth and increased fluency.]

Johannessen, Larry R., Elizabeth A. Kahn, and Carolyn Calhoun Walter. Designing and Sequencing Prewriting Activities. Urbana, IL: NCTE, 1982. [Series of cognitive exercises for teaching definition--formulating positive, contrastive, and borderline cases.]

Kneupper, Charles. "Teaching Argument: An Introduction to the Toulmin Model." CCC 29 (October 1978): 237-41. [Useful introduction to Toulmin system.]

Lunsford, Andrea A., and Lisa S. Ede. "On Distinctions between Classical and Modern Rhetoric." In Essays on Classical Rhetoric and Modern Discourse. Eds. Robert J. Connors, Lisa S. Ede, and Andrea A. Lunsford. Carbondale, IL.: Southern Illinois UP, 1984. [Excellent overview of differences between classical and modern conceptions of " t r u t h " a nd hence of argument.]

Perelman, Chaim. _The Realm of Rhetoric_. Trans. William Kluback. 1977; Notre Dame, IN: U. of Notre Dame Press, 1982. [Landmark of the "new rhetoric"; stresses tentativeness of argument--arguers don't prove; at best they increase adherence to a point of view.]

Perelman, Chaim, and L. Olbrechts-Tyteca. _The New Rhetoric: A Treatise on Argumentation_. Trans. John Wilkinson and Purcell Weaver. 1958; Notre Dame, IN: U. of Notre Dame Press, 1969. [In cataloguing ways that arguments can work, this text has had a major influence on contemporary discourse theory.]

Raymond, James C. "Enthymemes, Examples, and Rhetorical Method." In _Essays on Classical Rhetoric and Modern Discourse_. Eds. Robert J. Connors, Lisa S. Ede, and Andrea A. Lunsford. Carbondale, IL: Southern Illinois UP, 1984. [Excellent explanation of the relationship between an enthymeme and the values of an audience.]

Toulmin, Stephen. _The Uses of Argument_. New York: Cambridge UP, 1964. [General theory of argumentation shaping our approach to invention.]

Young, Richard E., Alton L. Becker, and Kenneth L. Pike. _Rhetoric: Discovery and Change_. New York: Harcourt, Brace and World, 1970. [Influenced our conception of the "new rhetoric"; introduced us to Rogerian argument.]

NOTES

NOTES

NOTES

NOTES

NOTES

NOTES

NOTES

NOTES

NOTES

NOTES

NOTES

NOTES

NOTES

NOTES

NOTES